THE TENSION POINT

Breaking Through
To Where You Want To Be

Harold Elmore & Kim Fletcher

ALOHA
PUBLISHING

"The book is easy to read and understand. It is challenging with the interactive exercises. The readers are encouraged to dig deep into their own minds to find what is really important to them. Your book is a great tool to help them find their 'why.'"

–Bill Davis, *My Daily Director, The Lifestyle Planner*

"The Tension Point is an insightful book. It takes the reader on a journey toward discovering identity and clarifying vision and is permeated with practical steps for creating a solid foundation to live a life of personal and professional confidence and success."

–Rebecca L. Carter, Executive Vice President, *Studio Q Furniture*

"One of the most powerful books I have ever read. Please read every word. Let the words and concepts absorb into the core of your being. This book will change your thinking, leaving you well on your way to discovering your authentic self and unleashing your true potential."

–Denise Horn, Professional Life Coach

"I truly believe that *The Tension Point* will help many find their true selves and, in the process, become all that God intends for them to be through the insights you have captured."

–Jane Gillen, *Vollara* Diamond

"I have known Kim Fletcher for almost 20 years and she has always lived with the ideals captured in this book. She has helped me see past my own limited vision and take chances I might not have, had she not been there to encourage me, whether it was in Ghana, West Africa, giving away wheelchairs, or in a conversation on her back porch sipping lemonade. She is a visionary who will empower you to be the same."

–John Wern, Director Special Projects,
Joni and Friends International Disability Center

"If you want to know who you are and why you are here to be a success, then this book is a must-read."

–Jon L. Estes, Pastor

"I'm convinced there is nothing more important than vision to compel someone toward success. Having a strong vision for my life has carried me through a devastating, paralyzing accident to become an inspirational speaker and wheelchair athlete. Kim Fletcher's coaching has been invaluable to me. *The Tension Point* will help you establish a clear vision and allow you to realize your dreams even in the face of challenging circumstances and obstacles."

–Stacy James, *Professional Inspirational Speaker and wheelchair athlete*

"I must say this is remarkable!!! Wow ... it is great." –Elaine Krieger

"I was transformed by the end of the first chapter! A must-read for everyone, at any age, who has the desire to take flight and be the brilliant person God intends them to be."

–Cheri Van Houten, Director of Marketing,
Joni and Friends International Disability Center

"*The Tension Point* should be at the top of your reading list for anyone who wishes to explore what true success is all about. As a Life Coach and as a friend, I consider Kim Fletcher to be one of the greatest influences on both my personal and professional life. She is a person of great integrity and passion."

–Rich Hallstrom, Founder and Host, *Motivation with a Purpose Radio*

"For the past 40 years, I have worked as a teacher, administrator, and also an educational consultant for the 6th largest school district in the United States. During that time I read many books on vision and leadership. *The Tension Point* will take a leader of any industry to the next level, moving you beyond all that holds you back."

–Ronald L. Clodfelter, Retired Principal, *Coral Springs High School*

"Great book packed with life-changing ideas! *The Tension Point* creates a path to the success you want for yourself. It helps you move out of your comfort zone and become the person you were meant to be."
–Dr. Steve Willen, DC, CCSP, *Willen Health*

ISBN: 978-1-61206-017-0

Cover and interior design: by Mercy Hope, mercy@mercyhope.com

Published by:
ALOHA
PUBLISHING
AlohaPublishing.com

Printed in the United States of America

First Edition

DEDICATION

<u>Harold Elmore</u>
I dedicate this book to my Dad, ***Rollin Elmore,***
who passed away June 5, 2007.
He taught me many sustaining lessons, including:
common sense isn't that common;
if your word is no good, you're no good;
and the value of hard work.
He will always be missed.

Thank you for the lessons, Dad!

<u>Kim Fletcher</u>
I dedicate this book to my friend, ***Lorrie Lawrence.***
Together, we have discovered the gateway into
the clearing where our lives can take on
light, freedom, and perspective.

By example, your life has brought *transformation* to mine.
You empower me to see Jesus in every place.

"THERE COMES A SPECIAL MOMENT IN EVERYONE'S LIFE,
A MOMENT FOR WHICH THAT PERSON WAS BORN.
THAT SPECIAL OPPORTUNITY, WHEN HE SEIZES IT,
WILL FULFILL HIS MISSION—A MISSION FOR WHICH
HE IS UNIQUELY QUALIFIED. IN THAT MOMENT,
HE FINDS GREATNESS. IT IS HIS FINEST HOUR."

—*Winston Churchill*

TABLE OF CONTENTS

Word from the Authors

Harold Elmore
Entrepreneur, Executive Trainer, and Former Pilot

I have always loved to fly; never content to be a passenger. For me, the joy of flying comes from being in command of the cockpit as pilot. In my forty-nine years of experience as a private pilot, I have logged many hours. Some yielded stories I still laugh at, others continue to take my breath away many years later, due to what could have happened.

Life as a pilot is a perfect picture of life on the edge—taking your skill and pushing it far beyond what you once believed possible.

Perhaps the greatest gift that I received from those hours logged in the air are the parallel lessons that apply effortlessly to living a life of vision and hope, in life and at the office. Therein lies my heart in bringing you *The Tension Point*.

I realized along the way that we each come to numerous points of tension; places where we must decide whether to press through and break out of our own comfort zones, or give up and settle in—a decision that often leaves us feeling stuck.

My personal journey has decorated me with many sales and business awards, along with the opportunity to train numerous highly skilled business leaders.

This book is my cumulative journey, where I sought to attain success only to find, time and time again, that I had actually sabotaged my own achievement. The following pages contain strategies and systems that any person—from high-level executives to college students—can easily adopt. They are powerful tools for anyone interested in crafting and living a life of true vision.

The Tension Point will hold no value for the person content to live life as a "passenger," easily content with the mediocre status quo. This book is meant for the brave of heart—those who long to "pilot" their own visions, pushing the limits of their potential, natural abilities, skills, and dreams in everyday life.

Unfortunately, I spent too much of my life not really knowing who I was or what I wanted out of life. I realized through the power of Coaching and soul searching that I had been trying to fit my life into a pre-made mold, crafted partly out of society's demands, partly out of a desire to please others, and partly out of my own wrong thinking.

With the realization that my life needed to be about much more than I had made it, I made many changes.

I realized that it wasn't my life's place to change me—it was my place to influence my own life. Life will change you, and too often it will do so in ways you did not want or anticipate—especially if you base your life on externals such as status, achievement, degrees, and awards. Externals may also include past failures, places you missed the mark. The accumulation of this "external thinking" can cause us to react impulsively, making choices and choosing directions that derail our intended destinies.

The shift I made moved me from a life governed by externals, to a life guided by the internal power of a right identity, a deep faith, my life's unique calling, and the vision that naturally flows out of those discoveries. My identity began to come into focus—the man I was created to become. As I got to know this new man, I began thinking about things long forgotten, things I had always wanted to accomplish. My days began to be filled with vision, permeated and shaped by my faith in God, for my life, and for my growing business.

As I stopped living someone else's life, the one I had taken on along the way, I started really loving my own life. I even celebrated by purchasing a new Harley Davidson and reconnecting to my old love of riding. These days, if I get stumped at work, I just head out the door for a mind-clearing, heart-renewing ride—something the old me would have considered irresponsible and extravagant. Interestingly enough, I now find that I am my most productive when I take time to connect to my passions.

The Tension Point is my ultimate exercise of what has become my greatest passion—*helping others.* I love equipping people for true success in life and business out of the years of wisdom I have collected via my own achievements, struggles, and incredible network of Coaches and Associates who continue to sharpen me to this day.

I am a pilot at heart, a man who loves to fly, and the greatest joy a pilot ever experiences is the honor of taking others along for the journey.

I invite you to pin on your wings and get ready for some soul searching. I will provide well-worn strategies and even the Coaching from my own Life and Business Coach, Kim Fletcher, my co-author of *The Tension Point.* Together, we will combine life and business success strategies with powerful Coaching tips that will allow you to craft and live out your own vision.

All you have to do is decide that today is your day to fly! Don't make the mistake I did, yielding too many years to empty pursuits that leave you discouraged at the end of the day. You were meant to live out a life of extraordinary vision as unique as your own fingerprint. Stop settling and join me for the takeoff, flight, and landing of a lifetime.

Word from the Authors

Kim Fletcher
Master Life Coach, Speaker/Trainer, and Three-time Author

One of my greatest joys in life is seeing individuals, whether friends or clients, come to the realization that their lives were intended to be about much more than they once had imagined … *they were made for a life of vision.* At this place of discovery, something amazing begins to take place. Passions, creativity, and innovative ideas appear almost effortlessly. From this place of unique personal vision, they press through to take hold of life's greatest adventure—the journey toward a life of deep faith, the only place where it is possible to discover your true life calling.

Almost daily, someone will ask me, *"What is Life Coaching?"* No problem, that is about as easy to explain as answering why the sky is blue. Like the sky, the "color" of coaching changes to meet each individual client's need. Coaching from client-to-client, and even from session-to-session with the same client, changes along with the color of the sky.

In *The Tension Point,* I have been given a rare opportunity. Instead of trying to explain the complex dynamic and potential results of Life Coaching without a meaningful context, I get to introduce you to one of my clients who took hold of the process of coaching and training as if his life and business visions depended upon it. As a result, his determination to activate what he has learned has brought true transformation to his personal and professional life.

My co-author, Harold Elmore, is a gifted and passionate entrepreneur, executive trainer, and private pilot. His business successes were many when we met. He has excelled in most of his endeavors including sales, business ownership, flying planes, and motorcycle racing. Yet, with many stories, awards, and accolades in his possession, Harold sought out a Life Coach because something was missing.

This book is a collective effort, bringing you a unique compilation of life experiences (successes and transparent challenges), professional skills, tips on entrepreneurship, coaching strategies, and over ten years of my revelations around the topics of identity, vision, personal account-ability, life calling, leadership, and restoration.

We realized that we shared the desire to compile these powerful strategies, systems, and fresh new perspectives which have transformed our lives into a book you could hold, read, and choose to activate in your own life.

You and I were designed for freedom, yet our automated world has turned us into beings who have lost our bearings and our greatest ambitions. We have traded personal development for performance and perfectionism. We have traded our authority and power, allowing ourselves to be controlled and shaped by cultural norms and the expectations of others. We have traded our unique identities and callings in life for a pursuit of status, position, and financial gain. We have traded in our own unique life path for a cookie-cutter version that leaves us feeling stuck, lost, discouraged, depressed, and hopeless.

Every time we try to break free and change, an invisible wall of "tension" seems to hold us at bay. Desiring the path of least resistance, we back off from our destinies and settle in for a long camping excursion at a location known as status quo.

If you are fed up with those who have told you that dreams do not come true or that your life has no real meaning, then this book is for you.

If your heart beats wildly as you ponder what is most valuable and important to you, a life of vision is for you.

If you are hungry to discover how you can pass along your own insights and strategies from the place of your own success, then the life of a visionary leader is for you.

INTRODUCTION

The Origin of The Tension Point
By Kim Fletcher

I remember the day well. My client, Harold Elmore, called in for a coaching session. He had been hard at work refining his vision for his life and his business, while creating powerful strategies that would move him from dreamer to achiever. He was not even aware of the most powerful shift taking place. This once self-assured man was becoming coachable, teachable, trainable—the mark of an individual who is determined to become all he was created to be.

In reply to a coaching question, Harold shared a glimpse into his imagination. This seasoned entrepreneur and executive trainer once had another dream—the dream of being a commercial pilot. When a couple of minor physical limitations eliminated him from the hard draft, he was left to dream of what it would be like to fly one of those massive jets. That lingering thought brought about this returning image that would play like a movie in his mind.

It was 6:15 a.m. as he settled into seat 7A and followed the flight attendant's command to fasten seatbelts and turn off all electronic devices. He abruptly ended his call to his wife with a quick, *"I love you, honey, see you tomorrow after the meeting."*

As the Boeing 747 took off, Harold closed his eyes and began envisioning the day—thinking through what it would take to close the deal and how great it would feel to return home with another successful business venture in place. The furthest thing from his mind was the dramatic interruption that would disrupt his plans and present one of the greatest challenges of his life. This challenge would come at 30,000 feet in the air, somewhere between Greensboro and Chicago.

His eyes opened abruptly as the flight attendant came over the loudspeaker in a voice that could not fully disguise her panic, *"Is there another pilot onboard?"*

At this moment, Harold snapped back to reality to realize he was actually sitting in his office chair (not on that 747), caught up in a vision that captured the mind of this private pilot many times before … *what if he was flying on a commercial flight when the pilots became disabled and needed emergency assistance? Would he be willing to step up and put all he knew of flying into practice when hundreds of lives hung in the balance? If willing, would the skills he had gained flying small planes be enough to save him and the hundreds onboard?*

He went on to say that he always reached the same conclusion—*"I would have nothing to lose and everything to gain in trying, especially if no one else answered the call!"*

"I WOULD HAVE NOTHING TO LOSE AND EVERYTHING TO GAIN IN TRYING ..."

As quickly as Harold could unfold this intriguing and imaginative story, my mind was filling with all of the parallels between this fictional journey and our journey toward a life of vision. Without realizing it, the outline for this book was created that day. As our dialogue continued, the session took us beyond the flying of a great airliner that Harold dreamed about, to making the strong application of his story to his real life.

Therefore, it was a highly personal coaching session that laid the foundation for the book you are holding. The idea for placing these concepts in your hands and heart came out of our mutual desire to equip and empower greatness in your life and to inspire your pursuit of a lifestyle-supporting business.

Our chapter titles emerged from the parallels we discussed that day; we believe they hold key strategies and systems that will allow any individual to craft and live out their ultimate vision.

Here are the vision parallels that will be invaluable as you seek to live out your unique dreams:

Chapter 1: Prepare for Your Moment of Decision

In this chapter, we will challenge you to reach the same conclusion Harold reached when the flight attendant sent out a plea for another pilot to step forward: he would have nothing to lose and everything to gain. Without him, the plane would certainly go down. With him, there was a chance of bringing that fateful flight plan to a successful landing.

As it pertains to your unique vision for your own life, you have nothing to lose and everything to gain. As you position yourself for your moment of decision, you will be empowered to solidify your identity, craft your vision, and take ownership.

Chapter 2: Activate Your Vision

When Harold made the heart-wrenching decision to leave seat 7A for the pilot's chair, he imagined a life-altering decision. The momentum set forth by the decision had the power to change the entire course of his life—and the hundreds of other lives.

As he took his new seat in the cockpit, he glanced back longingly at his past location. As a private pilot, he had dreamt of flying a large commercial airliner for many years, but not under these circumstances. As he secured his new position, he was immediately overwhelmed with the complexity of the cockpit.

He faced his fears as he realized this change of position was about to require commitment that would challenge the depths of his skill and confidence. *"Do I really want to commit"* was no longer a legitimate question; he had answered the call, and now nearly 200 onlookers expected him to come through on their behalf.

As soon as he verbally identified himself as "pilot" to the panicked flight attendant, it was time to take ownership with a heightened sense of responsibility. All there was left to do now was fly the plane to safety. He began immediately envisioning the landing to come.

Harold now had to activate his intent to fly. Your parallel: as you step into your vision and begin steering your life from this new vantage point, you will be faced with fear, anxiety, and an overwhelming desire to call for support. This chapter will enable you to shift from owning your vision, to actually committing to that vision's completion, all while engaging your natural gifting and the power of accountability as key strategies for flying out your dream.

Chapter 3: The Power of Momentum

Picture Harold taking his seat and putting on his headset. His first act as pilot was to connect by radio to the crew in the tower. He began to identify and think through every gauge and control that looked familiar to him as a small plane pilot.

Planes were not designed for takeoff. They were designed for flying. The great majority of fuel is burned getting those large, flying cities off the ground. Once they are airborne, they fly on momentum, burning a fraction of the fuel required to lift off.

Passion is to the visionary what jet fuel is to a 747. A pilot can possess all of the skill in the world, but without fuel, he will not be

> PASSION IS TO THE VISIONARY WHAT JET FUEL IS TO A 747.

taking off. Without passion, your vision will not have the fuel it needs to sustain it to completion. In this chapter, you will learn how to reignite your buried passions, reframe past failures as keys to success, and recharge your vision without losing momentum.

Chapter 4: Ultimate Focus Required

As Harold listened intently to the instructions from the experienced pilot on the ground, he had to focus with his complete mental and physical capacity on acclimating to the cockpit and controls. For the first time, he took a deep breath and realized he was actually flying this massive jet. His confidence began to build as he forged a relationship with the crew in the tower.

Pilots do not have the luxury of quitting midair. That would end in a crash. Too many visions, however, are abandoned mid-flight only to crash after a successful takeoff. You will be inspired to finish when others are bailing out, by putting key strategies in place to diffuse distractions, challenges, and obstacles. It will also enable you to build a support team long before you need them.

Chapter 5: Live and Lead with Vision

Things began to happen quickly as Harold prepared for landing. As directed, he put the flaps down and began slowing down on the approach. He watched his air speed closely. He had waited for this moment since climbing into the cockpit. As he pulled back on the yoke and prepared to land, he mentally walked himself through the landing.

Can you think of a vision you long to complete? Perhaps it pertains to your business or your family. A key lesson to be learned from pilots is the importance of envisioning the landing long before it takes place. This chapter will compel you to move beyond mere goals and dreams, to a lifestyle of vision—living today as if your greatest visions are already reality. This lifestyle will awaken the leader within. Times of celebration and restoration are essential to refuel for your next flight plan.

THIS BOOK IS UNIQUE
TO MOST ANY OTHER BOOK
WE HAVE ENCOUNTERED ON GOALS,
VISION, AND LIFESTYLE ENTREPRENEURSHIP.
PART OF THE UNIQUENESS LIES IN
THE POWERFUL MERGING OF OUR
YEARS OF BUSINESS OWNERSHIP,
INNOVATIVE PROFESSIONAL STRATEGIES,
LIFE COACHING INSIGHTS, EXECUTIVE
TRAINING, AND OUR OWN JOURNEYS FROM
DREAMER TO VISION ACHIEVER.

OUR GREATEST HOPE IS THAT YOU WILL BE
AWAKENED TO FULLY DEVELOPING
THE AMAZING PERSON INSIDE OF YOU,
EMBRACING YOUR FULL POTENTIAL,
CRAFTING VISIONS WHICH ARE
ANCHORED TO YOUR DEEPEST LIFE CALLINGS,
ENGAGING YOUR NATURAL GIFTING EFFORTLESSLY,
AND FLYING OUT A GRANDER FLIGHT PLAN
THAN YOU EVER DREAMED POSSIBLE.

SO CLOSE YOUR EYES, LEAN BACK,
AND TAKE THE PILOT'S SEAT.
YOUR DAYS OF IMAGINING ARE OVER.
IT IS NOW TIME TO ACTIVATE
AND LIVE OUT YOUR VISION.

Chapter 1

Prepare for Your Moment of Decision

The Power of Identity

"We generally change ourselves for one of two reasons: inspiration or desperation."   *—Jim Rohn*

Unfortunately, I spent too much of my life not really knowing who I was or what I wanted out of life. Something desperately needed to change. I came to realize that I had been trying to fit my life into a pre-made mold, crafted partly out of society's demands, partly out of a desire to please others, and partly out of my own misguided thinking. I had convinced myself that this is what it looked like to be a success. There was only one problem. I was not fulfilled or full of vision.

A powerful season of soul searching led me to hire my own personal Life Coach, my co-author, Kim Fletcher.

I began to open my eyes to the possibility that there may be more waiting for me than I had once dreamed. I had not been without external successes. At an early age, I became a licensed pilot. I also began collecting a series of professional awards and accolades in the business world, particularly in the areas of sales and training. But none of this "success" ended up having much meaning. My search drove me to take an honest appraisal of my life, my work, my goals, and where my current actions would take me down the road, if nothing were to change. I did not like what I saw coming.

My first thought was, I need to change some things about my life, but my Life Coach was quick to put on the brakes of this process—I was trying to accelerate prematurely.

She began walking me through a process of revisiting who I believe myself to be. Hours were spent discussing identity—the man I saw in the mirror, and the man I could envision becoming as my days flowed into years.

Much of this process felt painfully slow. At times, I thought she might be missing the point. After all, she was coaching a man who was already successful in many regards; he just needed to figure out how to feel a bit better about it all at the end of the day.

Today, I am a different man.

Along the way, two powerful things took place that changed everything for me. First of all, I realized that the most important achievement I would ever accomplish was to get to know the real Harold and begin to honor my own story, living out who God had created me to be. Out of this crucial place of a right identity, my coach assured me, would begin to flow rivers of vision and fulfillment—the things I had been seeking but could not seem to lay hold of.

The second thing that happened was this revelation: while I was hoping to change (improve) my life, my life had actually begun secretly changing me ... and it did so without my permission!

I took back the authority. I realized that instead of my life changing me, I could be changing and influencing my own life.

Let me offer a stern warning from a place of deep compassion. Life will change you, and too often it will change you in ways you did not want or anticipate—especially if you base your life on externals such as status, achievement, degrees, and awards. Externals may also include past failures or places where you missed the mark. The accumulation of this "external thinking" can cause you to react impulsively, making decisions and choosing directions that derail your intended destiny.

I would love to tell you that my roadblock was the massive amount of success that had gone to my head. But the applause of my successes to date was being drowned out by another series of voices. It actually turned out to be my past hurts, lingering fears, a deep sense that I would disappoint those closest to me; a plaguing doubt over whether or not I was, or could ever be, "good enough" filled my days insidiously, quietly, almost like a whisper.

Doubts about myself—and some well-worn, limiting beliefs—were placed on me by some real, and some perceived, circumstances. Events long since past were telling me who I was … and many of them were lying!

My self-doubt led me to set business goals and life visions that were what I thought they should be, not what I really wanted them to be.

My Life Coach reminded me that we are each the sum of those with whom we associate, so she began encouraging me to revisit some of my mentors, heroes, and friends who have inspired and equipped me.

At the top of my list, you will always find Zig Ziglar. When you hear that name, you instantly picture a man who is "successful" by any standard. But in his bestselling book, *See You at the Top,* Zig paints a powerful picture of his humble beginning:

> "After two-and-one-half years of less than overwhelming sales success (to be honest I wasn't even a whelming success), the picture changed dramatically and my career did a 180-degree turn. Here's the story. I attended an all-day training session in Charlotte, North

Carolina, conducted by P. C. Merrell of Nashville, Tennessee. It was a good session, but I have long since forgotten the specific techniques I learned. Later that evening I drove back home to Lancaster, South Carolina, to conduct a dinner demonstration. I was late getting home and even later getting to bed; then the baby kept us up most of the night. At 5:30 a.m. the alarm clock sounded off and force of habit rolled me out of bed. We lived in a small, upstairs apartment over a grocery store. More asleep than awake, I looked out the window and saw snow falling. There were already several inches of snow on the ground and I was driving a heaterless Crosley automobile. I did what any intelligent human being would do that morning. That's right, I crawled back into bed.

As I lay there it dawned on me that I had never missed or ever been late for a meeting of any kind. Besides, when they hired me—after my two month campaign to get the job—I had promised to attend all sales meetings and training sessions. Mother's words also came back to me. 'If your word is no good, eventually you will be no good,' and 'When you work for someone—work for them all the way. If you are in something, get all the way in and if you can't get all the way in—get all the way out.' I stumbled back out of bed and made that cold drive to Charlotte and a whole new way of life.

When the training session was over, Mr. Merrell quietly took me aside and said, 'You know, Zig, I've been watching you for two and a half years, and I have never seen such a waste.' (Now, friends, that will get your attention.) Somewhat startled, I asked what he meant. He explained, 'You have a lot of ability. You could be a great one and maybe even become a national champion.' Naturally, I was flattered, but a little skeptical, so I asked if he really meant it. He assured me, 'Zig, there is no doubt in my mind if you really went to work on an organized schedule, and started believing in yourself, you could go all the way to the top.'

To tell the truth, when those words really soaked in I was stunned. You have to understand my background to appreciate what those words meant to me. As a boy I was rather small, weighing less than 120 pounds fully dressed when I entered my senior class in high school. Most of the time since the fifth grade I had worked after school and on Saturdays, and hadn't been active in sports. My self-image was that of a little guy from a little town, who someday was going to go back to that little town and earn $5,117 in a single year. Now, all of a sudden, here's a man whom I admired and respected telling me, 'You could be a great one.' Fortunately, I believed Mr. Merrell and started thinking like a champion, acting like a champion, seeing myself as a champion—and performing like a champion."

Like Zig Ziglar, I have come to realize that how we view ourselves—on our best days and especially on our worst days—will determine much about our lives.

I will go one step further. I have come to believe that how you see yourself will determine who you become. Most books and resources that teach goal setting, and even living out bigger visions, leave out a critical element—the power of identity.

Vision doesn't come from our efforts … it is birthed in the depths of authentic hearts that have done the hard work of getting in touch with "who you are and what you are truly capable of."

The first goal in *The Tension Point* is to empower you to press through any tension points created in your current life by a wrong picture you may have established of who you are and where you are headed.

I have to laugh now because in the beginning of my own "coaching process," I wasn't very coachable. Looking back, I wanted to start achieving more right away and made a powerful and humbling decision, the decision to become coachable. This simple decision turned a hard piece of clay into a sponge, ready to absorb all I could from every person and resource of value to me.

Today, I am a coachable, softened spirit ready to take on the world. Here is the best part: the vision, mission, and goals I hired a coach to help me accomplish now come to me almost effortlessly. Along the way, I have become a man of vision and I cannot imagine any other life.

One of the tension points that could have robbed me of this great adventure I am on was my own mental and emotional baggage I insisted on taking everywhere with me. It was weighing me down and robbing me of vital creative energy. I now travel light, pressing through and working to forgive, let go, and get free! Even forgiving myself was an unexpected part of my identity journey.

The most effective path toward a life of great vision and achievement begins with "first steps first." In fact, Zig Ziglar once again nailed a powerful truth when he said, *"The person who won't take the first step is not likely to ever take the second or the third steps either."*

I have asked Kim to coach you through some of the wisdom she brought to me regarding this first step in your breakthrough process.

Know Who You Are and What You Are Truly Capable Of

"We need to remember man is designed for accomplishment; he's engineered for success; he's endowed with the seeds of greatness." –Zig Ziglar

When one refers to "playing your part," it almost sounds as if we are talking about nailing your favorite role in a play being offered by your local community theater. To play a part implies being offered a script to learn, and then acting it out flawlessly on stage for a group of onlookers or the audience.

Unfortunately, while playing a role in a play can be entertaining, far too many people actually live their lives this way. Many of us feel as if, somewhere along the way, we unknowingly stopped being our true selves and started playing someone else's part.

While it may be okay to act out a character for a few weeks as an actor or actress, the fun would cease the minute you were told you now had to play that part for the rest of your life, laying down your own identity to live out a character created for the stage or the big screen. We would be quick to refuse such a ridiculous request.

So why don't more of us stop at that point where our days, our activities, our lives begin to feel foreign, like we woke up wearing someone else's pajamas? Why don't we question what is going on that is making us feel stuck, fake, disappointed, disillusioned, and unhappy?

We have been taught to "keep on keeping on." Life comes at you hard, but you gotta just press on. We have been conditioned to believe that life gets harder as we age, mature, and gain some success—but is that our inevitable reality? Or is there something we can do to reclaim the best of ourselves?

Let's attempt to identify our first crucial tension point. I believe that at some point in time, most of us face this place of having lost sight of who we want to become. This makes it hard, if not impossible, to figure out what we should be doing with our days. What if part of what is feeling so hard is actually coming from within our own spirits? What if we could do something simple that would put us back on track toward becoming all we were created for and realizing, more than ever, that we are capable of far more than we ever dreamed possible?

But we keep on listening to the lies, the voices that tell us the mature thing to do is take the promotion, even though it will turn a forty-hour work week into sixty plus. We may hate the thought of coming home so late at night, but it is the "right thing" to do.

Regardless of the type or magnitude of the decisions being made, I can promise you a guaranteed result. Making decisions and life choices aligned with a faulty or incomplete personal identity (which, incidentally, shapes your professional identity) will lead you down a path where you ultimately wake up one day and realize you are no longer living out the life you were destined for. Rather, you have taken on a role, playing a character crafted out of past expectations and experiences.

For many, who you were destined to become has been derailed—most of us never get off of this crazy, fast-paced ride called life long enough to ponder who we long to become and what will be necessary to get us there … what thought patterns need to change, what limiting beliefs need to be abandoned—once and for all, what actions and behaviors are sabotaging our intended destinations?

Again, another tension point often presents itself here: *Will I live my life blaming those who have tarnished my destiny—or, will I stand up and do the hard work of forgiveness and letting go required to take back my destiny?* The work of clarifying your identity and determining what you have been placed on this planet to do cannot be done by anyone but *you.* You can blame others all you want, but the blame process will only tie you more closely to the lies.

It is time to let go of some things. At this empty-handed place, you are ready to receive some divine downloads about who you were really meant to become. Brace yourself, because getting in touch with who you are will begin to reveal what you are truly capable of becoming. This is the place where personal responsibility and a sense of deep meaning begin to flood every task you set out to accomplish.

Vision and confidence will flood over you and, much like land after a tsunami hits, the landscape of your life will be forever changed.

Proceed with great anticipation. The life about to be laid out for you is only for the brave of heart, those ready to live lives that surpass their wildest imaginations. It is intended for the adventure-filled minority who dare to put more emphasis on who they are becoming than on what they hope to achieve.

Identity—Discovering the Missing Element

"Our deepest fear is not that we are inadequate. Our deepest fear is that we are powerful beyond measure. It is our light, not our darkness that most frightens us. We ask ourselves, 'Who am I to be brilliant, gorgeous, talented, and fabulous?' Actually, who are you not to be? YOU ARE A CHILD OF GOD. Your playing small does not serve the world. There is nothing enlightened about shrinking so that other people won't feel insecure around you. We were born to manifest the glory that is within us. And as we let our light shine we unconsciously give other people permission to do the same. As we are liberated from our own fear, our presence automatically liberates others." Quote attributed to Nelson Mandela & Marianne Williamson

Arguably, there are multiple great books and resources that compel us toward living a life filled with vision, at the office and in our personal lives. However, while coaching hundreds of individuals over the past decade, I have found a common missing link among those whose visions continue to elude them leaving them frustrated, and surrendered to merely existing rather than living fully.

Identity is a key missing element in the crafting and living out of many great life and business visions. In fact, it is a key missing element in our culture. To be more clear, identity is not typically absent. Rather, our true identities have been replaced by broken and counterfeit versions. What is actually missing are the identities many were meant to possess—they've been tarnished, damaged, disfigured, and distorted by life.

This great omission certainly affects the person whose identity has been impacted by the past, but it also creates a ripple effect that impacts the world around that individual. I honestly believe that the world is cheated out of that person's greatness. The world we see breaking down around us is doing so, in part, because people simply do not realize the divine and powerful purposes for which they were created, so they design self-absorbed lives—losing sight of the greater good within them, that the world desperately needs.

To awaken to our own unique identity is to also awaken to the state of things around us and to what we have to contribute. But until we awaken, our lives will continue to be stifled, and our potential will never be fully reached.

If you don't believe that most people have no idea

about their unique identities, try asking someone who they are. The answers typically reveal roles and jobs, degrees and awards, or failures, losses, and disappointments. Within most answers, we cannot find even a modicum of internal significance. Personality, character, passions of the heart, natural giftings, and values are neglected.

We have become a sea of "doers" who don't know how to "be." We act more like preprogrammed robots than holistic, individual beings. This leaves us with the empty belief that we are what we do or fail to do.

Revolutionize Your Thinking

When we live focused on what we are doing and achieving, we surrender to an incomplete identity that is formed by the external elements discussed above, such as status, awards, failures, losses. This belief system sets us up for an inevitable crash, as life holds many undesired and unexpected changes. For the person whose identity is rooted in what he is accomplishing, imagine what will happen to his world in the event he loses that high-paying job, or sustains an injury that leaves him disabled and unable to return to his successful career. The world built on the shaky foundation of externals alone would be rocked.

Is there a way to guard against a total collapse of our identity when life comes at us fast? *We say "yes."* It begins by returning to a solid belief that the true essence of who we are is deeply rooted in the internal elements that are enduring and unchanging, and therefore cannot be stolen from us in times of crisis or challenge.

Our culture is replete with examples that point to the value placed upon doing and achieving. Individuals are commended who are overworked and always busy; multitaskers are seen as our modern-day geniuses. Those of us who work at a different pace, taking ample time to reflect and reconnect to passions and priorities, are often labeled as lazy or as underachievers.

So, let's begin our journey by establishing a few truths that seem to escape many individuals today. Research shows that as many as eighty percent of all Americans give little to no attention to this issue of identity. Most individuals invest their time, energy, and resources in achieving, accomplishing, and competing. While these qualities are admirable in the right context, the individual I want you to come to understand is the one who rushes forward, doing things with little thought to who he is becoming.

To further establish our disconnect with this issue of identity, take a quick moment to consider how most people in your immediate circle of influence would answer the simple question, *"Who are you?"* Most will quickly begin to reflect on their roles—parent, executive, tennis champ, runner, etc. Take your inquiry one step further and ask, *"No, I don't want to know your roles. Tell me who you are apart from those roles."* You'll lose most people right there, getting a blank stare and a mumbled, *"Well then, I don't know."*

Here is our premise as we launch out to craft a solid identity as the first step toward success: you can amass great success without being fulfilled. This type of success only leaves you feeling disillusioned and discouraged. This has often been referred to as ending up "unhappily successful."

If you wish to cultivate success that is fulfilling to you as a unique individual, you must take the position of the "successful minority" (the 20 percent) who begin all quests at the point of cultivating a strong, personal identity.

Many have set out to go after big visions, only to find that the completion of the "dream" left them feeling empty and confused. Here are a few key reasons to consider starting with developing you, rather than your goals, as your first step toward living a life of vision. Here are just a few of the many benefits of life lived in this order:

• When discovering your identity comes before your vision(s) for achievement, you will become more aware of all you are truly capable of.

- Ideas and visions that align with your passion, values, and purpose will seek and find you. You won't have to seek them.

- You will save countless dollars and hours by not pursuing training in the wrong areas.

- Opportunities will begin to come your way, giving you fresh chances to put your personal best into practice.

- You will begin enjoying the "sweet spot'" of living out of a place of purpose and significance, not mere achievement.

- Your life will be filled with few to no regrets, as your decisions and choices will begin reflecting who you want to become and where you want to lead those who are choosing to follow you as their leader.

- You will become empowered by a quiet confidence of knowing that the essence of who you are is unshakable and unchanging, allowing you to survive setbacks from external circumstances that cannot be controlled, such as economic challenges, changes in your industry, downsizing that comes along just months before being fully vested in your retirement.

- You just might find yourself being a sought-after expert in your industry. Individuals who possess a solid identity are comfortable with themselves, instantly putting others at ease.

Chances are you have picked up this book because you are interested in building the life and business of your dreams. You would not be reading along unless you possessed a deep desire to succeed as you define success.

The hard work of clarifying and correcting your identity will create a solid foundation upon which you can build a life of fulfillment and significance.

Identity is foundational for a reason. Think of the building you are in as you read these words (if you are blessed to be outdoors, imagine the closest building). You can see most of the structure above the ground, but the foundation is not immediately visible—it is underground. It is not glamorous, but it is essential. In fact, no builder or architect would argue, the foundation is the most important part of that structure. The foundation has to be aligned and constructed with precision or the integrity of the building will be threatened—the building could even crumble to the ground under minimal stress of a storm or other natural disaster.

Our great desire is for you to build upon your dreams and vision for life and work in a manner that will stand the test of time—creating a powerful legacy to guide generations to come. If you want to build a life that lasts, the foundation is the place to begin, and it should be constructed thoughtfully, carefully, and with great attention to detail.

Let's get started constructing:

Identity Forming Exercise

Begin by asking yourself this simple question: *"Who am I?"* Go ahead and include your roles, as these are key places where priorities and current skills will come into play.

Now, take it one step deeper and see if you can answer this simple question without regard to roles. As you strip away the roles (parent, friend, CEO, etc.), you will only be left with characteristics. Your awards, achievements, even your failures, don't have a place on this list either—so go deep. If you are having difficulty, here is a simple exercise: take a journal or legal pad. Write out the letters of the alphabet, leaving room after each letter. Then for each letter of the alphabet, complete a word that describes you. Pay no attention to things on your list that you don't love. Be completely honest with yourself. You'll have room to shift from who you are to who you long to become next, so don't worry if you feel change is in order.

Alphabet Exercize

- A—AMAZING
- B—BOLD
- C—CALM
- D—DISTINGUISHED

Finish by creating a word that describes you for all twenty-six letters.

After completing your list of twenty-six characteristics, go back with a highlighter or pen. Circle or highlight the ten that best define you right now. Hold onto those as your TOP 10 LIST!

Now, let's change the exercise slightly.

Go back to your blank list of letters. This time, as you create a new list of characteristics, answer this key question, *"WHO DO I LONG TO BECOME?"*

Now, follow the same step above and highlight your TOP 10 BECOMING LIST.

This exercise may seem simple, but it is designed to allow you some time to reflect, thereby:

- Allowing you to have a clearer picture of who you are right now.

- Designing your hope for the future as you consider who you long to become.

- Strengthening your belief in yourself by separating the roles and achievements from the unshakable heart of who you have been created to be.

- Forcing you to redefine and shift your core foundations onto who you are becoming rather than what you are achieving.

- Creating a place of stability as you begin to trust in who you are, something that cannot be shaken—even in times of uncertainty, crisis, or hardship.

No building can be crafted without a location, a piece of land, a place to stand. Your enduring "real estate" is your unique identity. This is the property you have been entrusted to steward, just as your home sits on your unique plot of land. As you build this solid foundation, you will have positioned yourself to build, achieve, and accomplish those things that will have lasting meaning, stability, and integrity as you venture forward in life. We all envy those homes and buildings that have the perfect location; for me, that would be an oceanfront lot.

Crafting your identity is like choosing the prime location or lot upon which to build the rest of your life. You get to choose who you are becoming, just like a person of wealth can choose where to build a home. If we follow that logic through, a quick way to become wealthy, in the truest sense of the word, is to choose to become someone you love—building the life you have been dreaming of.

Simply put, crafting a lasting and solid identity— one that reflects the best of your own heart—will give you a foundation upon which a life of true greatness can be crafted, one that stands the tests of time. Moving forward with a strong belief in yourself will allow you to enjoy stability, comfort, and ease of living that diffuses stress and anxiety as unexpected obstacles present themselves.

Those things we put into writing mean far more than those things we merely think or talk about, so let's finish this section with a simple writing exercise.

Are you ready to declare this new identity?

You can instantly think of numerous companies, teams, and even individuals who have vision and mission statements, but how many people do you know have their own unique identity statements? How can you know what you have been put here to do if you don't first come to know who you actually are becoming?

Complete this simple exercise, giving it serious consideration. Your answers will come from the alphabet exercise you just performed.

Simply fill in the blanks for a rough draft of your IDENTITY STATEMENT. Then feel free to change the wording, making it personal and meaningful.

Once crafted, put it where you can see it, repeat it, and memorize it. I like having this on a mirror, in my car, or even in front of my daily calendar. Have some fun by doing this exercise with your friends, children, and associates after you craft your own.

Fill in the blanks with your top three choices from the first two questions found above:

"I AM _____,

_____, _____.

I AM BECOMING _____,

_____, _____.

My identity is so important that I vow to align all future decisions and actions with who I long to become."

Signature:_____

Date:_____.

Congratulations! You are taking key steps that will position you for a great future by embracing the value of identity. Understanding who you are and who you are becoming naturally positions you for the next step, discovering what is truly important to you. As we begin to dive into this next section, allow yourself to begin considering what matters most to you right now in life.

As your true identity begins to be awakened, it will be natural and effortless for you to begin discovering what really means the most to you and what you are most interested in accomplishing. Do your "identity work" first. Lay that critical foundation and get ready to build upon it as you move toward crafting a life of vision and significance.

The work you have done already is guaranteed to bring you more joy than the perfect oceanfront property ever could.

Goals are Good, Vision is Better

"If you don't know where you are going, you will probably end up somewhere else." –Lawrence J. Peter

It's important you get clear about what you want and where you are headed. No one will argue with the simple fact that goals are good. People who set them tend to be more focused and more successful than those who do not. But I find that many people who seek out coaching or training for their professional development often overlook the bigger picture of where their goals are taking them. In doing so, they overlook the greater truth: *while goals are good, vision is better.*

Goals will certainly allow you to take steps toward a specific accomplishment, whether you desire to gain a new professional certification or lose twenty pounds. But if that goal is not framed in the context of a much bigger and more compelling picture, it may never come to pass. New Year's resolutions are the perfect illustration— millions of people set them with good intentions, and most fail to keep them. Why? Goals should not be seen as an end result in and of themselves. Rather, I like to call them action steps—steps that are taking me where I long to go.

That goal of losing weight can quickly cause me to feel deprived when it stands alone, dictating my eating and exercise routine. But when that goal is a mere stepping stone—I began to picture myself more thin, more healthy, and full of energy—something changes. The bigger picture of vision shows me where I am headed before I ever arrive. I begin envisioning the "new me," which, in turn, begins motivating me from a positive place, rather than a lifestyle of restraint. (That, by the way, is why diet is a four letter word in my vocabulary; it tells me what I will lose, but leaves out what I will gain—and by gain, I am not referring to weight!)

The most powerful part of vision is that it ties our intentional steps (goals) to the benefits that await us as we reach our desired destination. My goals have become effective and respected steps that I honor as I view them within the context of where they are taking me. Steps that feel like drudgery become a bit less painful and boring when I realize they are exactly what is required if I am to reach the place of success I can see in my mind.

Goals were once all I had to motivate me out on the road as I traveled from business transaction to business transaction. But today, I am motivated by a much grander vision of where my goals have the ability to take me if I engage my power and take these key action steps daily and consistently (we will discuss more about the power of consistency in chapter 5).

Stop for a moment and consider your current goals. Are they written down? Do you have a clear picture of why you have crafted them? Where are they taking you? Are they set within the bigger picture of all you stand to gain as you hold to them faithfully?

If this is not clear, take a step back and spend some time considering where it is you are headed—and where you want to end up. Some adjustments in your vision may be needed. Once your desired destination becomes clearer, you can more easily design the steps that will be most effective in taking you there.

This simple illustration from *Full Steam Ahead!*, by Ken Blanchard and Jesse Stoner, supports our point on the power of vision, with goals positioned as action steps moving you toward your desired destination:

> "The expression *full steam ahead* comes down from the days of steamships when it meant the powerful ships were moving ahead full force. Today, full steam ahead means being so clear about your purpose, so committed to it, so sure about its importance, and so sure about your ability to accomplish it, that you are able to take decisive action despite obstacles. In our book this expression described the effect of having a clear vision—knowing who you are, where you're going, and what will guide your journey—fully powered to move ahead full force. In order for organizations

to be fully powered, the leaders need to know how to create a compelling vision that resonates with the hopes and dreams of those in the organization. Leadership is about going somewhere. If not in service of a shared vision, leadership can become self-serving."

They go beyond talk about individuals in this illustration to also address the power vision has to change the entire dynamics of a team. Vision and shared vision are at the heart of the world's most successful companies, the happiest families, and the most dynamic individuals.

Take a moment to coach yourself with a few questions which test the effectiveness of your current vision:

- Has your vision been worked out at the heart level?

- Have you moved beyond impressing and pleasing others to reaching for a vision that belongs solely to you?

- Does your current vision energize and motivate you?

- Do you wake up excited, realizing you are one day closer to achieving all your vision encompasses?

- Are the benefits associated with your vision completion clear to you?

If you find yourself answering "no" to any of these simple questions, this may indicate a need for a short vision sabbatical. Take all you can afford, whether it is a long coffee break or a full week. Get alone with your heart, and begin crafting and refining a vision that resonates at the heart and compels you into action.

Some people go through life without vision because they mistake it as a process only for those who are interested in "extreme success," such as becoming a millionaire, retiring by thirty-five, inventing a hot-selling product, or owning a ten-thousand-square-foot home. Let me say, for the record, that is simply not true.

In the book of Proverbs, God's own voice is captured when He states, *"Without vision, men perish"* (Proverbs 29:18). This simple statement holds a profound truth: vision is for everyone! Without it, we merely exist, walking out days that seem to steal the life right out of our being, little by little.

It is time to redefine "extreme success." For me, extreme success is doing life on my own terms. I set the schedule; I determine how many days, weeks, even months, of vacation I take per year; I decide where my efforts will take me. I press on to make the most out of this life I have been given.

This "extreme success" is a way of life intended for each and every one of us—especially for you! But it is only available to those who live from the vantage point of vision.

Finding a vision will require taking time to listen to yourself. Understand what it is you desire out of life. What have you been good at in the past that might show you what you might be great at in the future? It's there for a reason. Our experiences to date hold many clues as to our highest gifting. Even our greatest challenges can sharpen us for the journey when they are held in the context of our supreme visions.

Balance Your Goals

"Vision creates focus. Vision identifies direction. Vision unleashes power." –Ken Blanchard & Jesse Stoner, *Full Steam Ahead!*

Can you quickly state your priorities? Do they reflect a balanced representation of both the personal and professional sides of your life?

Imagine your goals on a large scale—personal goals on one side, professional goals on the other. When most people take a look at their goals, they find they are being more intentional in one area of life, either personal or professional. If all of a person's goals are rooted in business accomplishments, that person will likely find their pursuit of degrees and promotions ultimately sabotaging their personal life, sending personal priorities way down the list of importance, or throwing them out of the picture altogether.

Our goals must be balanced!

Balanced goals take our bigger vision for our lives and fit our vision for professional pursuits in their right place. Balanced goals make sure we focus on what is truly important and keep us from forgetting about the people and things that matter most to us—our relationships and marriages, our kids and grandkids, our family and friends, our pursuit of wellness and health.

After many years spent pursuing financial success, I can tell you something profound—*financial success can only take you so far.* Money can only buy things. It cannot purchase all my vision encompasses. It cannot buy true peace, joy, health in relationships, or most of what really matters to me.

Take a word from someone who has learned a few things the hard way. Balance your goals now and give yourself permission to honor the priorities that deserve a high position in your heart. What is in your heart will be reflected by your actions. It is not enough to say that something or someone matters. Take time today to make sure your actions reflect what matters most.

A life that honors people first (this includes yourself), and things later will always bring greater fulfillment in the long run. It will even ensure that you have great people in your life who are ready and willing to celebrate your successes with you along the way.

The person who has moved from mere goals to true vision is a person whose priorities are intact and whose life is balanced in all areas, keeping first things first, and making time to celebrate along the way. The person of vision sees the coming benefits and realizes that today's sacrifices and commitments will be more than worth the effort. This individual has embraced the freedom to be his best. Now, what will we do with our freedom?

TAKE OWNERSHIP IN YOUR MOMENT OF DECISION

"Freedom to be your best means nothing unless you're willing to do your best." –Colin Powell

Now that we have done the work to discover our unique identities, we are each positioned to know more clearly what we are truly capable of. Reaching our full potential depends upon our ability to stay connected to and build upon our foundation of a strong and intact identity.

Once we begin to awaken to our true potential and full capabilities, we become ready to face key moments of decision.

As you are reading along, you may be considering a career change, a big move, whether to adopt a child, or one of many other key life decisions. Your decisions at this stage may be smaller ones. You may be considering how you should invest your day today, what to do about the tension that seems to be growing between you and your supervisor, or whether you should sign up for that free class at the local community college.

Either way, life presents us with key moments of decision. They come in all shapes and sizes. As we make decisions daily, we create actions which begin to direct our days, moving our lives down certain paths.

Every life decision, regardless of its perceived magnitude, should be filtered through this simple question: "Will this decision move me closer to my greater visions for life, or further away from it?" When I speak of this critical question, I'm assuming you have already answered the prerequisite question that is the essence of our identity discussion: *Will this decision move me toward or away from the person I believe I am to become?"*

I (Kim) attended a conference a few years ago taught by award-winning singer and songwriter Margaret Becker. She was teaching on life balance and one of her most powerful concepts was what she has come to call her *"Yes/No Template for Life."* She described that her life had gotten out of control, too busy from the overflow of "success" to stop and reconsider her direction. She took a self-imposed, one month sabbatical (and you thought I was crazy to suggest a week); during that month, this concept was one of her new revelations.

She vowed to begin living and working off of this *"Yes/No Template."* She simply asks herself, *"Will this decision, I am about to make, take me closer to my intended destination (her vision), and will it reinforce who I am striving to become (her identity, values, and priorities)?"* If the answer is yes, she considers saying yes to the decision at hand. If the answer is no, she moves beyond the decision with no regret, knowing it would have only taken her off course in her bigger vision. Today, this simple practice has allowed her to redirect many of her efforts to match her passions, allowing her to spend more time on those pursuits that match the desires of her heart.

Are you trying, or are you committing?

Most people go about setting goals and dreaming of greater achievement by saying, *"I will try this."* Here is one simple thought that may change your life: Those who "try" rarely succeed. Success is left for those who determine to "do it" rather than simply "try."

In his book, *The One Minute Manager,* Ken Blanchard says, *"There's a difference between interest and commitment. When you are interested in doing something, you do it only when it is convenient. When you are committed to something, you accept no excuses."*

Taking ownership of your vision for work and for life is the first step in the critical process of commitment. Because ownership and commitment are unique concepts, we will begin discussing ownership in this section, and will build into discussing commitment in the next section.

Taking ownership of an idea, vision, or desired achievement requires removing that little word filled with sabotage—try. So, as you face your current decision, set your face like flint and declare, "I will make this happen. I will succeed. There is no room for the word 'try' in this equation."

Just as we saw with Zig Ziglar's story early on, success will continue to escape you until you make a decision to be a success. Once I decided to launch the business I own today, I didn't keep looking for something better or give myself easy outs. I focused on my business and refused to look to the left or to the right.

Many people start a business or enter into a career transition with half-hearted effort while they keep looking for something better. This is the evidence of a person who has failed to find their niche in life. *Warning: do not recruit them to your team.* They are short-termers who will be easily swayed to other ventures, because they are not anchored to their own passionate vision.

You will need to accurately assess yourself before you will have the ability to discern where others are in this process of discovering and owning their own visions. If your vision and subsequent decisions do not currently capture your whole heart, stop and reassess. Otherwise, you will set yourself up for a disastrous fall. Few things are worse than ending up being successful at something that lacks meaning.

It is easy to "own" a vision that does indeed capture your entire heart and being. You will find yourself awakening to new possibilities and creative innovation as you step on the path and take full ownership of the direction you have chosen. This path is personal, it is fulfilling, and it just may lead to destinations better than you ever imagined.

An owner will determine how he treats something based upon its perceived value. A family heirloom diamond will receive different treatment than a chipped set of china purchased at a garage sale. In similar fashion, a young adult will place different value on the educational track they choose out of their passions, compared to that imposed and forced upon them by a parent or guardian.

You will only begin to take true ownership, and ascribe great value to your life and business visions, once you realize that next to your own identity, they are among your most valuable possessions.

To take this idea one step further, consider the idea of stewardship—the place where we are entrusted with the task of managing something that belongs to someone else.

I believe my life and my greatest visions come from, and ultimately belong to, God. He has entrusted them to me … and He is certainly more valuable than anything I will ever accomplish. Realizing that I steward my decisions, the health of my own identity, and the direction of my life makes all the difference as I seek to honor Him with my choices, behaviors, and what I choose to "own." From this vantage point of believing, my life does not belong to me, but ultimately belongs to God. It has been given to me to fulfill His great purposes; now I can make much of my life confidently and boldly … all the while pointing the credit back toward heaven as I enjoy this life of vision. There is another perk to this way of life. God has promised to empower and equip me for everything He has purposed for me to do. *You can't beat that guarantee.*

Stop today to consider what God has created you to do. What if you have been crafted with more capability and potential than you ever dreamed possible? How would your future moments of decision be altered if you viewed them from this unique perspective?

Treat Every Decision as if it is Life-defining

What would happen in your day-to-day life—whether at home or at the office—if you began to give significant weight to your key decisions? How would it change your direction, your commitment level if we began viewing every choice, every decision as life-defining, if not life-saving?

Another principle from scripture is the picture of the person who is faithful with the small things ultimately being entrusted with great things to steward. If you want to have great success making grand life decisions, we suggest you start by reframing your small decisions. We want to share an exercise that will get you in touch with the importance of the seemingly small decisions you make daily and how they ultimately position you to make the larger choices that perfectly align with your vision.

This simple exercise causes me to slow down and consider where I am headed. *"Do I stay at work this afternoon or head to my grandchild's soccer game?"* gets more attention than a passing thought. I actually stop to consider the outcome of this simple-seeming decision.

Small Descisions Given Big Weigth Exersise

Start by taking out your daily planner. Glance over your week.

Determine that in the week to come, you will take time at the beginning of each day to connect to the heart of this exercise. Most of us make small decisions with almost no thought at all; when we are feeling busy or overwhelmed, the urgency of the moment takes over, causing decisions that are quite important to be treated as if they are of no value.

Now, make a list of the "small decisions" you envision today holding: what will you have for lunch; what will you do with those twenty minutes between your two morning meetings; will you work late or find a way to get home in time for dinner with your family; will you keep that engagement with your friend or call to cancel because you are too busy?

The next step is a hard one: Look at each seemingly meaningless decision on your list and ask this question of each one, *"What is the easy decision and what is the right decision?"*

Now, structure the day to make the right decisions, making adjustments as necessary.

Congratulations, you have just spent an entire day choosing the important over the urgent. Now, expand this to include an entire week. Keep this up until it becomes habitual for you to stop and consider the outcome of your small decisions—decisions that were previously being made with little thought of how they connect to the big picture.

Those who give due weight to small things and small decisions begin to honor and reconnect to what is truly important, creating a powerful framework in which larger decisions can be made with clarity and focus.

When faced with the larger decisions, expand your coaching questions to include:

- Does this decision line up with and reinforce my priorities?

- Will it make me more productive in the long term?

- Will it reinforce my commitment to those I love?

- Does this decision move me closer to my ultimate dream and vision?

With this highly intentional method of decision-making, a new goal, refined vision, or potential business venture gets filtered through the context of *"how will this affect my life, those I love, and those who are choosing to follow me as leader? Will this decision I am about to make move me closer to fulfilling my daily goals and ultimate vision, or will it cause me to stray?"*

Even more importantly, *"will this step I am about to take move me deeper into the person I long to become, or will it derail my unique and powerful personal identity?"*

Since this is your company, your business, and your life—it has to be *your* decision. Also, your moments of decision must be met with the weight of *commitment* they are due if you are to see them to completion. By beginning to treat the small, daily decisions with high regard today, you will create a pattern that will carry over and allow you to make wise choices, rather than impulse reactions when the big decisions come your way tomorrow.

Take simple steps before acting. If you are considering starting a business or launching a new division, check the facts: make sure there's a viable market, and make

YOUR MOMENTS
OF DECISION
MUST BE MET WITH
THE WEIGHT OF
COMMITMENT
THEY ARE DUE

sure you and your team are positioned to offer something unique that will make you an asset and not a liability to your industry. Begin to craft ideas that will answer painful questions and meet key needs within your area of expertise to stay viable for the long range.

Your Business Identity

In the section on identity, we discussed the importance of crafting your personal identity. You must do the same with your company. Know who you are as a business entity—your uniqueness, your strengths, your passion.

Simply put, it will be impossible to craft an enduring business vision and make right decisions unless you know who you are within the business world, and what unique needs your company is positioned to impact.

Make sure your personal identity and your professional identity are something you really connect with at the heart level—attach yourself to causes, people, and ideas worth believing in for the long haul.

In my many years spent training sales people, I learned that if they don't believe in themselves and the product they represent, they might be successful for a few months, but they will soon drift away. You've got to believe in the product or service and be able to identify viable benefits that are potentially life changing for your customers and your team.

For your business to succeed long term and reward you with fulfillment, you need to believe that the services or products you offer make a key difference.

Crafting your business' identity statement will allow you to become more closely acquainted with who you are in the business world. Knowing more specifically who you are and what business needs you are equipped to meet will position you for your key moments of decision as you move forward toward your greater vision for your work days. Knowing who you are is critical as it will protect you from taking on ideas, responsibilities, and future plans that are not in keeping with who you are becoming professionally. This will simplify your days, reduce stress, and allow you to work more and more in the areas that come naturally to your unique gifting.

In summary, to increase your clarity around your key moments of decision, take the following simple steps:

• **Identity comes first.** Do the work to craft your personal and professional identity before you are faced with decisions which carry heavy consequences. Take time to write it out, sharing them with your team.

• **Practice powerful decision making.** Begin giving extra weight to small daily decisions to create the habit of responding rather than impulsively acting when big decisions come your way.

• **Increase your clarity around moments of decision.** Make choices which align with your priorities and your vision; ask yourself, *"Will this decision move me closer to or further away from my vision of who I am becoming and where I am headed?"*

• **Begin to test your vision to determine if it is compelling.** Your vision must be clear and in place before you will be able to use it as a filter for your key decisions.

We began with identity. As who you are becoming starts to come into clear focus, it is time to consider what you have been put here to do. Whether considering this from a personal or professional vantage point, what is most meaningful to you? When was the last time you stopped to ask yourself that simple yet powerful question?

What I have been put on earth at this time to specifically accomplish will naturally flow out of the person I am becoming. Just as identity positions us in life, gaining clarity around what we should be investing our best in begins to illuminate life and business visions that matter uniquely to us.

WHAT I HAVE BEEN PUT ON EARTH AT THIS TIME TO SPECIFICALLY ACCOMPLISH WILL NATURALLY FLOW OUT OF THE PERSON I AM BECOMING.

In fact, identity gives you a critical edge. Thomas Jefferson once stated, *"Nothing gives one person so much advantage over another as to remain cool and unruffled under all circumstances."* The best way to do this is to be grounded in ourselves and our ultimate purposes.

Identity continues to have a critical role as we move toward action because it gives us belief in our potential. We need to embrace our unlimited potential or we will likely choose goals and visions that are too small or lack personal significance. We might even find ourselves doing what others think we should, rather than honoring our own voice and vision. The people-pleasers among us could do the best job of writing to that issue!

Let's begin with a simple exercise that will get you in touch with what matters most to you right now. In the first section, you were encouraged to think more of your inner qualities and characteristics. In this section, we will take that next critical step toward considering who and what really matter most to us in life. Roles, goals, and vision evolve and change as our identity stays relatively solid (only hopefully becoming strengthened and enhanced along the way).

Make a list of your roles: *CEO, parent, friend, board member, etc.*

Now, consider the 3 "P's": *People, Priorities, Passions.*

Building life and business success with "no regrets" requires an honest appraisal of what is already in place in your life. Too often, a promotion or impulsive action takes a person toward great sounding rewards, while leading him further away from what he once valued most. To avoid the pain and mistakes associated with impulsive action, give yourself a few moments to put your future desires and dreams into the right context.

Make a list of the most important people in your life right now.

Of these people, circle or highlight the names of those you have committed to go the distance with (example: Your spouse, children, lifelong friends, etc.)

Make this list as long or short as you desire.

THE MOST IMPORTANT PEOPLE THAT I WANT
TO HONOR AND INCLUDE IN MY FUTURE INCLUDE:

1.

2.

3.

4.

5.

6.

7.

8.

9.

10.

Now make a list of your Top 10 current priorities.

MY TOP 10 PRIORITIES INCLUDE:

1.

2.

3.

4.

5.

6.

7.

8.

9.

10.

Finish by making a list of the things you are most passionate about.

This list might include things you love to do, places you love to visit, people you want to strengthen relationships with, causes you wish to participate in, skills you want to develop, music, art, or creative ventures.

I AM MOST PASSIONATE ABOUT:

1.

2.

3.

4.

5.

6.

7.

8.

9.

10.

Another way to consider your passions: they are the things that make you tick! *"I am in my element when_____."* (Make another list).

With ability comes responsibility. An honest appraisal of your identity—for your life and for the work you will contribute professionally—will pave the way for you to act with clarity when key moments of decision present themselves.

Ownership unlocks opportunity! The clearer you get about who you are meant to become, and what you have been placed here on earth to do, the more you will begin to recognize and embrace opportunities that have seemed to escape you in the past.

CHAPTER DISCOVERIES

- How we view ourselves will determine who we become and what we accomplish.

- Life will change you in ways you did not want or anticipate, if you base your life on the externals rather than on the internals of character, values, passions, and life calling.

- Reaching our full potential requires a strong and intact identity—in life and in business.

- Forgiveness and letting go must happen before you can live out your truest vision.

- It is a tragedy to amass great success and not be fulfilled.

- The clearer you become about your desired destination, the easier it becomes to create action steps that will lead you there.

- The most powerful decision-making tool lies in one simple question: Will this decision move me closer to my greater vision or further away from it?

- "Trying" is the enemy of "achieving."

TENSION POINTS

- Failing to clarify and strengthen your own identity

- Maintaining insecurities and lack of confidence

- Being unaware of your own potential

- Procrastinating

- Allowing impulsive decisions to sabotage your vision

- Lacking ownership of your own destiny

- Settling for a life of goals without vision

ACTIVATE YOUR COACHING BREAKTHROUGH

- Create one daily strategy to begin investing in the person you want to become.

- Consider your greatest "identity block"… now, turn it into a positive affirmation and begin reciting it daily. For example, the identity block for someone who feels not smart enough begins to say, "I have more than enough wisdom to accomplish my highest vision."

- What vision (future dream) do you hold deep inside of yourself that needs to "take off"?

- What simple steps could you begin taking so that each day moves you closer to that vision?

CHAPTER 2
Activate Your Vision

COMMIT TO YOUR UNIQUE VISION

"Whatever you vividly imagine, ardently desire, sincerely believe, and enthusiastically act upon ... must inevitably come to pass!"
—Paul J. Meyer

"We have nothing to lose and everything to gain." That is the mantra and ultimate hope of every person who commits to seeing something through. Once you have taken ownership of a vision or an idea, it is time to press in and get fully committed.

The first step in committing to your unique visions for work and life, is crafting a vision that really means something to you personally. For many years, I found myself coaching others to avoid trying to pursue someone else's dream. It just does not work, as that path leaves you disillusioned and frustrated every time—despite the amount of success you achieve along the way.

Just this past year, I found myself having to take my

own hard advice. I had gotten caught up in the excitement and prestige of a grand new goal that enticed me. An opportunity with our company got my heart pumping as I reminisced about sales and business awards and records of years past. *"I could do that again and be a great success,"* I thought to myself. I revised my mission and vision statements to align with this lofty new goal; and, for a time, I anticipated "winning."

But all too soon, the excitement was replaced by a lack of focus and anxiety. I began to feel pressured to succeed. Increased tension began to rob my days of joy. I had worked so hard crafting my mission and vision statements—what had gone wrong? I sat myself down and reviewed my business plan, my goals, my values … ah-ha, there it was. Somewhere along the way, I had made the very mistake I warned others to avoid.

I had taken on a new venture without weighing it against my priorities, my values, my business and personal identity, and my enduring mission/vision statements. This goal that had caused me to redirect my focus and attention was not my goal. It was simply a good goal with great potential that I should have said no to!

I went to work immediately reconstructing my vision and omitting this grand goal that was derailing my plans. That does not mean I won't try to reach lofty goals in business. It means the only ones I am ever going to have a strong chance of bringing to completion are the ones that hold deep, personal meaning and tap into my natural abilities. This allows work to feel almost effortless at times, and tension and anxiety are unusual occurrences rather than my day-to-day reality.

There are going to be numerous moments of decision, as opportunities come your way. The key is going to be deciding which ones line up with your ultimate vision and which ones may seem good at the time, but prove to be distractions down the road.

In his book, *Visioneering*, Andy Stanley defines vision this way, *"Vision is a clear mental picture of what could be, fueled by the belief that it should be."*

Two little words: could and should. The true vision keeper will toss out many "could be" decisions along the way, always making room for the "should be" decisions.

What we should be doing is again driven by that deep inner knowing of who we are and what we have been gifted to accomplish. Once you determine what you should be doing and who you should be becoming, the next step will flow naturally ... taking ownership and committing to your vision.

In the scenario I shared earlier, as a private pilot, I began imagining what would unfold if I were ever to be on a commercial airliner when the pilots became disabled and someone was needed to safely land the plane.

In that moment, as I stood up and identified myself as a pilot to the flight attendant, I was taking ownership of the fact that I was willing to assist in the crisis. Ownership is the first step toward commitment, as it shifts us into a place of responsibility and accountability. Ownership implies possession, and possession implies that we are holding something of value.

Commitment is the path taken by one who determines to take that thing of value—whether a vision for business or wedding vows—and see it through at any cost. This is the point where we must press into our vision with everything within us.

This story gives powerful insight into the distinction between the dreamer and the achiever. The dreamer goes at life with less than 100 percent effort, thinking a lot about what might take place; the achiever settles in and presses the throttle to 100 percent capacity, determined for his vision to takeoff.

Ownership takes place in a moment. *"That is mine. That belongs to me. I will purchase that."* On the other hand, commitment is the long range proof that we value what we took ownership of as we stick with it and see it through.

This one simple principle has the power to set you apart in a culture of quick fixes, instant gratification, and haste to abandon any ship that is not yielding the promised results.

The minute we take ownership of an idea, a principle, or a life decision, we are often immediately faced with doubt and anxiety.

Can you imagine what would have been going through my mind if I really had abandoned seat 7A on that flight for the pilot's seat? I would have been shooting down doubts as fast as they could sail toward my mind.

Will I be able to pull this off? Do I even want to? Is this really for me? These questions lead us to either make a strong commitment to that which we have taken ownership, or to abandon it.

When you start a business or set out toward a new vision, you may initially end up with more questions than answers, because there is no way a book or teacher can impart to you everything you need to know about cultivating great business success. But take heart. Answers will begin to emerge as you begin taking consistent and committed steps toward the bigger picture that is coming to view in your mind.

I have learned a critical lesson piloting many successful flights. When flying (and life) gets crazy, it is time to bring order to our desired achievements. Bringing order to the situation proves to be one of the most powerful tools for dispelling anxiety and moving the situation toward a successful resolution.

Regardless of your current position, whether you are sitting on the edge of a new venture or well down the path toward your vision, there are a few things you can do to clarify and simplify the journey.

IF YOU HAVE A VISION FOR YOUR LIFE OR BUSINESS THAT IS WORTH ACHIEVING, IT WILL LIKELY LEAVE YOU FEELING OVERWHELMED AT TIMES.

If you have a vision for your life or business that is worth achieving, it will likely leave you feeling overwhelmed at times. One way to stay committed on the hard days is to simplify your approach while also taking certain, ordered steps.

If you have ever flown a plane, or listened in as a pilot prepares for takeoff, you recognize the orderly process of checking instruments and planning out the voyage. Each step is taken in order, with great attention to detail. If a problem or doubt is encountered, it is handled before heading onto the next step. Takeoff never occurs until certain items are in place, checked, and deemed safe.

To ensure the success of your growing visions, I suggest following the daily practices of any accomplished pilot … bringing order to the takeoff phase.

In *Teach Your Team to Fish,* Business Consultant Laurie Beth Jones encourages readers to simplify, quantify, and multiply as they put forth effort to expand their visions and hone their teams. She writes out three simple steps:

1. **SIMPLIFY**—get to the essence of what you came here to do.

2. **QUANTIFY**—determine ways in which progress will be measured.

3. **MULTIPLY**—ensure that everyone on the team has the ability to multiply the good of the organization through every contact they make.

Simplification begins with knowing who you are and who you are becoming. As we become clear about who we long to become, we will be able to clarify what we have come to accomplish, those things that are most meaningful to us.

Vast visions are seldom accomplished alone. This is where we must begin to multiply—adding team members, vision-keepers, encouragers, and accountability partners to our journey.

As we learned from the expertise of pilots, never allow your vision to takeoff until you first simplify your goals and vision (concentrating on what matters most);

quantify ways you will track your progress; and set a plan in place for communicating with, and staying connected to, your team of co-visioneers.

Currently, I (Harold) sell the world's leading technology in air purification, as well as recruit and train members of the key sales team. The company has tried and tested proven methods for success. The wise recruits follow this time-tested wisdom with precision.

First, I teach sales trainees to ask key questions to determine the flow of their days. To understand and clarify the steps for success, you will also need to ask questions specific to your business vision.

The following questions assist my trainees to gain clarity around their unique sales goals:

1. What path will you take? Start by taking ownership of the professional path you are on.

2. What are the benefits, for you, your team, and your customers? Knowing the benefits of your product or service allows you to proceed with excitement and integrity.

3. If you are going to sell a certain piece of equipment such as air purifiers, how much inventory do you need to have on hand?

4. How much volume do you need to sell to meet your sales goals?

5. What is your business strategy? Once you determine the volume of sales needed, you must create a strategy for succeeding at that goal. Perhaps, as with this company, you know you will likely sell 50 percent of the equipment that you are allowed to demonstrate for potential customers. This insight makes it easy to lay out a daily, weekly, and monthly strategy to grow your business.

6. Are you adding team members to assist you? You will need to develop a team building strategy that runs parallel to your sales strategy.

While your particular business or professional vision will be unique to you, you can take value away from this simple question-asking exercise. Take a few moments and make an orderly list of steps needed at various stages in your business development. The needs will differ for those just starting out, those well into the process, and those now considering building their business up to sell or turn over to a new leader.

On December 12, 1977, I received an award given by a company called *Goodwill Association* out of Gastonia, North Carolina. It was called the CSR—*Certified Special Representative award*. It was awarded to people who had a consistent twelve-week cycle of great production, based on both volume and quality of business. During that particular period of time I was totally focused on one thing: getting that CSR award.

I was hungry for this reward and I found myself picturing the exclusive ring on my finger, a symbol of success only awarded to the highest achievers. Just as in the example above, I took time to ask key questions. *What amount of sales will I need weekly? How will my typical goals have to be elevated during this twelve-week cycle?* I set my mind on the reward and spent my days with ultimate focus.

More than ever before, I was in the zone and ended up earning my new ring with two days left in the contest. I wore that ring for many years as a reminder of what is possible when we give our all. Commitment to my unique vision had seen me through to completion!

After winning the award, I drove straight through from Little Rock, Arkansas, to Sebring, Ohio. I didn't have much money at the time, so I had to travel conservatively. Stopping for a great night's sleep in a hotel was not an option. I arrived on a Sunday afternoon, in time for a church service. I showed up unshaven and scruffy. The minister approached me and asked if I would share my testimony. So I got up on stage and began to talk, which takes courage for a sleep-deprived individual.

Part of my vision for those twelve weeks was to get back in time for that service. Without passion and strong desire I wouldn't have made it. In the message, I told a key part of my story. My vision for winning this award was actually linked to helping someone else succeed.

When my goal for succeeding created a partnership with my passion for helping others to achieve greatness, I gave my all effortlessly.

Never forget the power and passion that come when your visions for life and business reach beyond yourself, reaching out to empower and motivate those around you. That is what turns a successful business person into a true leader!

You must throw yourself wholeheartedly into the endeavor of your vision, determined to takeoff full throttle, holding nothing back. Once your wheels leave the ground in takeoff, you are fully committed. Now, all there is to do is fly that vision to a safe and timely landing. One of the most natural ways to thrive will be leveraging your natural abilities.

LEVERAGE YOUR NATURAL ABILITIES

"He found his mission in life by … doing something that came easily to him." –Laurie Beth Jones, *The Path*

Often, I think we are too quick to place skills and natural abilities into the same category. In fact, they are distinctly different; and confusing the two can have lasting consequences.

What are your truest strengths? Do you feel most gifted in the areas where you have invested time and resources studying to gain certain skills, or do you feel more gifted at those things that come naturally, with little training?

All too often in today's world, we find people working jobs for which they have been trained, while they enjoy hobbies in their free time which are rooted in their natural abilities. As a person who has trained numerous individuals for various jobs, I would recruit a naturally-gifted person in whom I must invest more training, to bring his skill-base in line with a particular job, any day, over a skilled person with high levels of training, who lacks a natural bent toward the work they are doing.

Learning comes easily, flowing from the depths of a person's being, when we tap into our natural abilities. But all too often, the demands of life, and the need (or desire) for a certain level of income and lifestyle, leads many of us to pursue jobs and careers that are not even close to our natural gifting—leaving us at risk of burning out, feeling frustrated, and losing promotions to the guy or gal who "is such a natural."

If you have not already made this life-altering discovery, then today is your day to begin aligning your future career and business pursuits with how you are naturally gifted.

One key step in the process of breaking through to meaningful achievement is identifying and leveraging your natural abilities. While your natural abilities, also known as talents or natural giftings, can be strengthened with training and discipline, they exist and come forth as naturally as the color of your eyes. You will execute them with ease. In fact, they may come so naturally, you have a hard time identifying them, just as you fail to count the times you take a breath or the number of times your heart beats in a day.

Here is a great way to begin discovering your natural abilities so you can leverage them for great success: eavesdrop on what others say about you. You may find others commenting, *"You are really great at_____." "You are a true natural." "I wish that came as naturally for me as it seems to for you."*

Begin by asking those closest to you what they see you being truly gifted at. Also, ask yourself this revealing question: *"I am in my element when_____."* (Review your answers from the Identity section.)

Many people grow frustrated in life because they chose a professional path that requires great skill which is not connected to their natural gifting. While we may learn just about any skill, skill does not connect to our innate passions and purposes the way our natural gifts do. We are hard-wired internally with identity, natural abilities, and passionate purposes that are as unique as our fingerprints.

Because your natural abilities are a gift God hard-wired into the depth of your being, they will be the easiest to develop and will give you the greatest sense of fulfillment as you operate within them.

In *The Path*, Laurie Beth Jones shares a powerful story of how a man found his true mission in life by giving freely of his natural gifting:

> "The famous Santa Fe artist and woodcarver Ben Ortega was a farmer who, as a hobby, used to carve wooden saints. One day the community held a fund-raising craft fair, and he donated one of his hobby carvings of St. Francis. So many people ordered the piece that he had to quit farming and take up carving full-time to meet the demand. He found his mission in life by giving what he loved away—doing something that came easily to him."

Take a minute to complete the "Hobby & Contribution Test". Grab a legal pad and make two columns. Title one HOBBY & CONTRIBUTION and title the second column WORK TASKS.

Get ready to fill in column one, the HOBBY & CONTRIBUTION column. Think about what you are currently doing with your volunteer service time and your free time, the time you use to give back and to refocus and refuel. If your work schedule leaves you too busy to volunteer or have hobbies, simply ask yourself what you would do if you had free time. What activities have you participated in over the years leave you with the greatest sense of fulfillment or satisfaction? Perhaps it was volunteering for a humanitarian building project, or offering free consulting to a local not-for-profit organization. Perhaps it is a week spent annually at your favorite destination, or teaching a child to fly a kite.

Now begin filling in the second column, WORK TASKS. Here you want to include the typical tasks that fill your days in order to fulfill your job description.

Here is where the test gets hard … take time to see how the two columns line up. Is there any overlap in what you invest in daily, compared to what you would invest in if you had more free time? Or do the two columns look as different as night and day?

There is something powerful to be learned from the life of Ben Ortega. Sadly, most people spend their days working in jobs and living out life in ways that require skills they have gained along the way, perhaps in the form of college degrees or advanced training programs. The training they have received has taken them down a path toward job security, but far from the natural abilities and passions of the heart.

If you are seeking to start a new business, reinvent some key area of life, or choose a career path, do yourself a tremendous favor—link your chosen profession and future vision to those things that come most naturally to you. This one step will position you to accomplish more, with less effort, while enjoying daily fulfillment.

Leveraging your natural abilities will help you connect daily to the person you were created to be. Giving away part of that gifting for the gain of others, rather than for personal gain, just may unlock a life-transforming opportunity.

SEAL THE COMMITMENT
WITH THE HIDDEN POWER OF ACCOUNTABILITY

"Personal accountability is about each of us holding ourselves accountable for our own thinking and behaviors and the results they produce." –John G. Miller, *The Question Behind the Question*

Recognize the Need for Help

Having taken the pilot's position for many flights, one of my (Harold) first thoughts upon occupying that seat of honor is to connect by radio to the air traffic controller. No matter how well I fly, I know that I am in need of a great team of support to bring each flight plan to a safe conclusion and a smooth landing. In fact, I could never say it better than Ken Blanchard, *"Feedback is the breakfast of champions."*

There is much to be learned by the powerful picture of a pilot in communication with the crew in the tower. In fact, I highly recommend recruiting your own team. While the air traffic control tower is full of flying experts, your tower will be full of different experts.

What does the current stage of your life and business require? Is your financial team in place? Do you have a good relationship with a business attorney? Have you ever tried the powerful process of life and business coaching, partnering with your own coach who is skilled to bring out your absolute best? Do you have the technical support needed to maximize the use of technology to grow your business? How about the one most people leave behind—the accountability partner?

Your team of vision keepers and accountability partners will journey with you as you walk toward your unique goals and visions. Ask yourself who will be willing to come alongside you—to help guide you toward your anticipated landing of your own great visions in a way that is firm, yet positive.

Get these key individuals in place long before you need them. You don't want to radio for help on a crucial day only to find that there is no one in the "tower" to answer your call for support. You also don't want to be the type of individual who only calls someone when you are in need of something. Take time to carefully choose members for your "tower" and begin valuing them long before you need them! Invest in them, support them, surprise them with notes or gifts of gratitude. Then, when you need them most, they will be quick to answer when you radio for assistance.

In chapter 4, we will discuss strategies for investing in your support team before you need them. Because accountability is so powerful, yet often avoided, we devote the rest of this section to these powerful partnerships.

The accountability partner is a key team member that most exclude on their journey toward success. Many are too prideful to be coachable or teachable … a sure shortcut to failing fast or ending up alone! Remember, I learned these lessons the hard way. Today, I have weekly contact with individuals positioned for the unique purpose of holding me in account of what I have committed to do. These trusted partners have quickly become some of the most important members on my team, as they have been entrusted with my most specific goals, visions, and tendencies to fail. They know how to hold me accountable in ways that work for my personality. They keep me sharp, committed, and focused, and I willingly share the glory with them at the end of the day.

As you recruit and strengthen your current accountability relationships, keep the relationship in the right order and perspective. Too many people put the weight on the one holding them accountable, but think about this:

In his book, *The Question Behind the Question,* John G. Miller makes an important distinction regarding the power of personal accountability. He teaches that while many companies, mastermind groups, and success advocates teach that accountability starts with the commitment of an accountability partner, in all actuality, accountability starts with the person receiving the accountability.

I must determine my own need for accountability and invite others to partner with me—to hold me accountable to the things I have deemed critical to my own success. While they function in a key role, the ultimate responsibility rests on me, not on them.

It has been proven that your likelihood of reaching a particular goal is less than 20 percent, even if you think it through and write it down. That percentage soars to over 80 percent when you take that goal, write it down, and then invite someone to hold you accountable for achieving it in a timely manner.

You will place yourself in the successful minority simply by having the humility to admit your need for support, then acting on this need by recruiting accountability partners. *In fact, your success will depend upon it.*

Accountability is not just in place to assure that you

have great success along the way. Success is a side benefit; the real fulfillment rests in making a difference along the way. In my opinion, the true power of accountability is its ability to ensure that I live out my God-intended impact in the spheres of influence where I have been placed.

Harry S. Truman once stated, *"You can accomplish anything in life, provided that you do not mind who gets the credit."* Accountability takes our ambition, and eyes, off of ourselves and links it to the greater good that will be achieved when our goal is reached. Get ready to share the glory with those who care enough to invest in your success.

Increase Your Account-Ability:

Before recruiting new accountability partners, do a bit of homework. Taking these simple steps will increase your Account-Ability:

• Position yourself as coachable and teachable. There is no need to waste anyone's valuable time and input if you know you are not able to learn from or take feedback from others. Stop here and get some support making this shift before moving forward. No matter how much you know, the journey will be lonely and empty if you allow pride and arrogance to isolate you from those who could be sharpening and encouraging you.

Special Note *to those who may be struggling for legitimate reasons: Some of us have been wounded in the past by verbal abusers and have isolated ourselves in self-protection. My friend, please get the support needed to counsel your way through this road block. While self-protection may keep some bad things away, it also repels a lot of good— including people who want to come alongside of you on this journey.*

- Make sure the person recruited is an appropriate person for holding you in account to a certain goal. If your spouse stresses over finances, he or she may not make the best partner for holding you accountable to your financial goals. You may have multiple accountability partners for your varying areas of goals and proposed achievement.

- Choose someone you respect highly and can take constructive feedback from without feeling defensive.

- Set regular times to meet and share how you need to be held accountable. This will vary according to your personality and needs to be personalized to fit the current need.

- Determine how you will proceed when your accountability partner identifies areas where you are slacking off, stuck, or apathetic.

- Watch for your responses to be filled with "I" statements, as true accountability will always fall back on you. Beginning your sentences with "he, she, or they" may indicate that you are making excuses or projecting blame.

- Fill your strategies with "how" and "what" statements and questions, rather than "why." The simple word "why" tends to put most people in a defensive mode, so train your accountability partner to ask you how you can accomplish something or what you need to do differently instead of hammering you with why you did not fulfill a commitment to a goal.

In *Working Wisdom: Top Ten Lists for Improving Your Business*, Thomas Leonard offers the following list of questions that will assist you in clarifying your accountability needs (the thoughts of the authors are in italics):

1. **Identify the exact desired outcome before taking the action.** *Be sure to share this detailed information with your accountability partners so they have a clear picture of where you are heading and what you believe it will take to get there.*

2. **Learn while you take action; improve and adjust what you do and how you do it.** *Invite their feedback if they discern areas where you should consider new or different actions. Making small adjustments along the way will keep you from veering far off course.*

3. **Take twice as many actions as you think it will take to get the results.** *Give your partners permission to be firm and raise the bar.*

4. **Make sure the actions you are taking are the ones that will get the results you want.** *Ask those coming alongside of you to help critically analyze whether your actions match your goals. Again, be open to their ideas on what might need to shift or be altered for you to succeed.*

5. **Make sure you are taking the "perfect actions," instead of just being "in action."** *I have often heard it said that practice does not make perfect. Perfect practice makes perfect. Your accountability partners are not there to force action; rather, they are there to hold you to the right actions being done consistently.*

6. **Make sure that every action you take produces at least some measurable result.** *One crucial way your accountability partner can support you is in creating ways to measure and track your progress—don't stop at talking this out. Make sure you create a paper trail of success by actually writing down your progress and any associated challenges.*

7. **Be willing to abandon your original objective if something better occurs.** *Your partner can keep you from going too far down a dead-end highway. Be open to input.*

8. **Make sure the actions you are taking affect others positively and add value to their lives.** *Invite close scrutiny on how your progress is affecting others. When we navigate through change, others can feel left out, inferior, insecure, and frustrated. To ensure true success, you must make sure to give an honest look at whether your actions, goals, and overall vision are impacting those around you in a positive manner, while you walk out every aspect in integrity.*

9. **Make sure you have all the resources you need to follow through when you take action.** *Your accountability partner may have resources or individuals within his or her network that will be strategic for your journey. As a side benefit, by opening up to someone, you also gain their network, wisdom, and experience.*

10. **Make sure that you are the right person to be taking these actions.** *One of the most important parts of accountability is the "should" factor. While we "could" take many actions and many paths, are we taking the ones that we "should" take? The should factor will allow your accountability partner to remind you to filter everything through the grid of your own identity and overall vision, and to only move in the directions which reinforce and develop who you long to become.*

Sharing simple guidelines, inspired by this list of questions, will allow you to develop accountability partnerships that will keep you honest and connected to your goals and visions, and accelerate your momentum and success. Don't forget to share the credit by encouraging and investing in those who willingly come alongside of you.

These simple steps will increase your Account-Ability and place you on the cutting edge of success in an ego-driven corporate climate.

CHAPTER DISCOVERIES

- The only vision worth committing to is one that holds deep personal meaning.

- Taking ownership of your vision is the first step toward fully committing to see it through.

- Vast visions that promise great reward will seldom be accomplished alone.

- Tapping into your natural abilities will enhance learning, motivation, and overall success.

- One great way to learn how you are naturally gifted is to ask those closest to you.

- Pride and insecurity are the greatest enemies of accountability.

- Accountability is a secret weapon for success, and it is only available to the person who is coachable.

TENSION POINTS

- Trying to live out someone else's vision or dream

- Thinking *"I will try"* brings success, when success requires *"I will do it"*

- Allowing important tasks to get crowded out by the urgent

- Investing in developing skills which do not connect to your natural gifting

- Remaining totally unaware of your natural abilities

- Permitting pride to cause you to avoid accountability

- Sabotaging your accountability by refusing to be coachable/teachable

ACTIVATE YOUR COACHING BREAKTHROUGH

- Identify one area where you have been thinking *"I will try"* and shift into full commitment with *"I will make this work."*

- Answer, *"I am in my element when _____."* What clue does your answer reveal about your natural gifting? How can you link that ability to your days?

- Name one urgent activity that robs your focus and keeps you from your most important tasks. Example: internet, phone time, dealing with complainers, etc. Set up a *"Do Not Disturb"* zone where you refuse to be distracted for a block of time each day.

- What is one area where you have refused coaching or accountability? *Today is the day to change!*

Chapter 3

The Power of Momentum

Passion Outperforms Skill

"A wonderful thing happens to people when they become passionate about something: they become proactive; they take initiative."

—Erwin Raphael McManus

In *Think and Grow Rich,* Napoleon Hill shares a story called: *The "Impossible" Ford V-8 motor.* It powerfully illustrates how passion trumps skill:

> "When Henry Ford decided to produce his famous V-8 motor, he chose to build an engine with the entire eight-cylinders cast in one block, and instructed his engineers to produce a design for the engine. The design was placed on paper, but the engineers agreed, to a man, that it was simply impossible to cast an eight-cylinder engine-block in one piece.
>
> Ford said, 'Produce it anyway.' 'But,' they replied, 'it's impossible!'

'Go ahead,' Ford commanded, 'and stay on the job until you succeed, no matter how much time is required.'

The engineers went ahead. There was nothing else for them to do if they were to remain on the Ford staff. Six months went by, nothing happened. Another six months passed, and still nothing happened. The engineers tried every conceivable plan to carry out the orders, but the goal seemed out of the question; 'impossible!'

At the end of the year Ford checked with his engineers, and again they informed him they had found no way to carry out his orders. 'Go right ahead,' said Ford, 'I want it, and I'll have it.' They went ahead, and then, as if by a stroke of magic, the secret was discovered.

The Ford determination had won once more!

This story may not be described with minute accuracy, but the sum and substance of it is correct.

Henry Ford was a success, because he understood and applied the principles of success. One of these is desire: knowing what one wants."

Where did that "Ford determination" come from? In one word, *passion*. Ford's passion for seeing his vision through caused him to press on when his engineers did not believe they possessed the skill to make it happen. What Napoleon Hill referred to as the "Ford determination" looks like passion to me.

Think about passion for a moment; not passion in the romantic sense (that is another book altogether), but passion in the sense of what drives you. What desires outweigh the rest? What pursuits leave you dreaming about the seemingly impossible?

Do you ever stop to think about the role passion plays in professional success? For that matter, do you ever give attention to those around you, some who seem content with mediocre achievement while others strive for excellence? Those striving for excellence tend to share a common ingredient: *passion*.

Passion, to me, is an excitement—it's a strong desire. It's a driving force that is more powerful than pain, suffering, and tiredness; it propels you to do what you need to do, even on the days when you really feel like giving up.

Jerry Gibson, a former boss and enduring friend, once told me if I could work by myself I would make a fortune. But he said, *"Harold, you are one of those people who works better helping people; that helps me make a fortune and you do okay."*

I love helping other people—I have discovered this one thing is my greatest business-related passion. I enjoy showing other people how to be successful. I get a real boost out of seeing others enjoy their own success. Knowing I have been part of many individuals' pursuit of business ownership, sales expertise, and re-designing their lifestyle creates an excitement that propels me further toward my own vision.

My (Harold) sales career started in 1973, working for a company called *Goodwill.* Within six months, I became one of their top trainers despite never selling anything before. Shortly after starting work at a land sales company, I was, again, quickly promoted to sales manager. I realize today many promotions I received actually existed to "promote my passion," placing me in positions with enough authority to assist, equip, and empower others.

Failure and Success are not Opposites

"Whether you think you can, or think you can't, you are usually right." –Henry Ford

Recently, I was asked to give a talk to a group of realtors about success. I told them for greater success they need to increase their number of failures. It was a foreign concept to most of them. They just didn't want to fail at all. In the speech, I focused on an important truth. Just as Ken Blanchard and Don Shula penned in *Everyone is a Coach*, *"Success is not forever and failure isn't fatal."* Until we can wrap our minds around this, we will take failure as a sign we should quit, instead of a sign that we are one failed idea closer to the idea that will bring about great results.

Many people don't realize that you actually fail your way to success. What I mean by this is simple: the number of failures to your credit does not determine your ultimate destiny. It only points to the number of times you have tried your best. Tom Hopkins says, *"I am not judged by the number of times I fail, but by the number of times I succeed, and number of times I succeed is in direct proportion to the number of times I can fail and keep on trying."*

To further highlight the importance of thinking rightly in regard to failure, I'm including an excerpt from *Maximum Achievement* by Brian Tracy:

"Thomas Edison was the most successful inventor of the modern age. He received patents for 1,093 inventions, 1,052 of which were brought into commercial production during his lifetime. But as an inventor, he was also the greatest failure of his age. He failed more times, in more experiments, attempting to develop more products, than any other living scientist or businessman. It took him more than 11,000 experiments alone before he finally discovered the carbon-impregnated filament that led to the production of the first electric light bulb.

There is a story about Edison that, after he had conducted more than 5,000 experiments, a young journalist came to him and asked him why he persisted in these experiments after failing more than 5,000 times. Edison is said to have replied, *'Young man, you don't understand how the world works. I have not failed at all. I have successfully identified 5,000 ways that will not work. That just puts me 5,000 ways closer to the way that will.'*

At their best, failures will clarify our abilities and vision as we move forward, creating momentum for success. At their worst, failures will cause us to stop and sit down, losing hope in ourselves and belief in our vision. Failure should give life to vision, but for many it kills it instead.

In his national bestselling book, *How to Become CEO,* Jeffrey Fox includes a compelling thought:

> "Companies are filled with idea killers. The idea killers come in all personalities, job titles, shapes, and sizes. The idea killers say things such as, 'We've tried that before,' 'management won't buy it,' 'we can't afford it,' and a hundred other anti-risk statements. One of the most common anti-action shots is the insufferable 'it won't work.' This is particularly frustrating because it usually comes from people both senior and experienced in the company."

I love his use of the words "anti-risk" and "anti-action." Idea killers can certainly be found lurking in the office or a cubicle next to us. But they can also be found inside of our own heads and hearts ... they especially love to take up residence in those places within ourselves where we hold onto doubts and fears that need to be put to death.

It is critical for any person who is serious about identifying and pressing through their ultimate tension points, while breaking through to great freedom and fulfillment, to let go of the false notion that failure is the opposite of success.

It is time to embrace the vision-altering, hope-infusing truth that failure is a critical ingredient that will be experienced by every person and every business that reaches a place of success. Please understand, we are not encouraging or condoning reckless conduct that harms yourself or others. Rather, we are encouraging you to be gentle with yourself when viewing past failures, walk in forgiveness toward others, and let go so you can move forward unencumbered for your journey toward deep and lasting success.

GUARD YOURSELF
FROM IDEA KILLERS

Guard yourself from idea killers; begin by making sure that one is not living inside of your own head or heart. They come in the form of:

- Negative thought patterns

- Doubt-driven self talk

- Past failures you desperately need to let go of

- Believing something false someone said about you

- Mistaking hardship and unforeseen challenges for your own personal failings

- Putting too much weight on a place where you failed to achieve what you hoped for

- Getting stuck in the past ... believing that your history equals your destiny

- Failing to forgive yourself at the points in time where you truly have failed to meet the mark set for yourself, in life and in business

- Failing to forgive others who have intentionally, or unintentionally (out of their own brokenness), sabotaged your success

Reframe Your Greatest Failures

Take a few moments before launching into the next chapter to do a bit of self-evaluation. Are there areas where you need to let go, forgive, reframe your thinking, and create new strategies for making perceived failures a part of your future success?

Here is a powerful exercise you can coach yourself through. Make a list of your perceived failures to date. Include your greatest regrets, failed investments, business ventures gone bad, key weaknesses, and the top five hardest tragedies or challenges you have faced so far.

Now, taking your list in hand, begin asking yourself what you have gained in those places where all felt lost. Make a list of the lessons learned, wisdom gained, insights sharpened, gratitude awakened. You see where this is headed. You single-handedly hold the power and authority to re-frame your past—allowing the wood, hay, and stubble to be burned in the fires of forgiveness, while moving forward with the pure gold and refined beauty that has emerged.

Too often, we miss the best of life's lessons when they come disguised as failures. I know a professional speaker who was lousy at his chosen profession. His limitations got him fired one time too many; no one in his small community would hire him. Out of sheer desperation, he moved and took up a new trade. He turned out to be so gifted at sales—the only job he could find in that town—he now travels the country teaching and training some of the world's most successful sales executives and business owners.

You will find great freedom, lightness, and joy as you move forward leaving the past in its rightful place … *far, far behind!*

Learn from your mistakes and leverage the challenges that others wrongly identify as impossibilities.

You are only as limited or as full of potential as the degree of belief you place in yourself, and by the number of times you are willing to keep pressing through when others tell you to throw in the towel.

If your vision still compels you, it is not time to quit. Rather it is time to press through. On the other side of your Tension Point awaits a new, fresh perspective on your life and your professional pursuits.

Recharge and Refine Your Vision Without Losing Momentum

"If there is hope in the future, there is power in the present." –John Maxwell

Definition of recharge: *reenergize, to charge again, replenish.*

Definition of refine: *improve by making small changes, remove unwanted elements, to bring a pure or fine state.*

Recharging and refining are keys to sustaining momentum as your dream pushes forward. I believe the most important step when recharging and refining your vision is to make sure it is *your* vision. I realize we have already touched on this, but it is important enough to mention again.

At least two times in my life I have taken on a vision that was not mine. I did it for all of the wrong reasons. After some soul-searching, each time I realized I was being drained of energy and losing momentum. When I redirected and refined my vision, the momentum returned.

When you have a vision that is truly yours, it can be easily sharpened and refined by setting exciting short-term goals. These short-range accomplishments can be put in place to move you toward your vision, while also giving you mile-markers of achievement to assist you in charting your progress.

As you reach those goals, be sure to have rewards in place, another key element in recharging. Choose rewards that are meaningful to you and be sure to follow through as you have promised yourself.

A self-imposed reward for achieving one of my recent business goals was an extra two weeks in Florida where I already had a short reservation. When I achieved it, I called to extend my reservation. Then an amazing thing took place. My vision took on greater clarity—the action steps required to move in that direction came into view with ease during that time of being unplugged and relaxed. I came away ready to move forward in boldness and passion. In other words, my "reward" became the catalyst for a huge wave of creativity and business growth that followed my time away.

Hope in the future comes from a clear vision that has gone through multiple layers of refinement. The power comes from the momentum which holds the drive to get you where you are headed. Trying to build a business or achieve a vision without momentum is like trying to steer a parked car.

When I attend a seminar or training, I notice most in attendance would already be considered successful. This gets me thinking every time. Successful people sustain the momentum of their success by going after more training, sharpening their tools for achieving. The reverse is also true. When you stop learning, discovering, and challenging yourself, the momentum begins to slow down and will eventually come to a screeching halt. A stopped vehicle rarely ever makes its ultimate destination.

I provide a training call for my current team every Monday night. The successful people—the people who don't necessarily need to be there—are the ones who inevitably show up consistently; the people who desperately need to be there aren't, because they think they already possess what they need to succeed.

Are you willing to do the preparation work required for taking you to the next level? If so, you will seek out the needed training and discipline yourself to take regular breaks for recharging and refining your ultimate visions. It has been said that President Truman died with an inspirational book under his pillow. *That is quite a picture.*

What is under your pillow right now?

Another great way to fuel your momentum is to get specific training and support. Training and seminars are often industry or topic specific and are limited when it comes to your specific vision. This is where coaching can play a crucial part in your overall success.

In her book, *Living Without Limits,* Judy Siegle, two-time paralympian and spinal cord injury survivor, has these remarks about her own experience with life-coaching and its role in taking her to the top as an elite wheelchair athlete who still holds four national records in wheelchair track today:

> "In her article, *'Deepening Your Learning—Life Coaching,'* Linda David says, *'to be both effective and fulfilled in our personal and professional lives today, we need to learn continuously about ourselves, other people, and the many facets of our businesses and our careers.'* We can continue to gain information and grow… through life coaching. Just as athletic coaches are respected as voices of experience, Life Coaches work with clients in all areas … clients set their goals and their coach works with them to meet and realize those goals. They form a partnership to develop the plan, implementing opportunities, strategies, and changes along the way. In 1996 on a flight from LA to Minneapolis, I found myself seated next to a woman who introduced me to the

concept of life coaching. When she discovered I was training for the Paralympics, she suggested that finding such a coach to help me prepare for the mental game would be beneficial. A Life Coach herself, she took me through a session I found very helpful, so I followed her advice and worked with a Life Coach for six months, honing my mental game in preparation for the competition in Sydney, Australia. Even though I had a great support team going into this training period, my Life Coach was someone I could talk with exclusively about the challenges of training at the elite international level.

Ann Gooding, a diplomat of the *American Psychotherapy Association*, says that life coaching is the fastest growing field, second only to management consultants, as people seek help and direction in order to lead more fulfilling lives."

I (Kim) am proud to call Judy Siegle one of my closest personal friends. I am also proud to have been included in her selection of Life Coaches at many points on her journey, as this former athlete now takes her message around the world as a professional motivational speaker. I share a clip of Judy's story for a reason. As a quadriplegic, no one would fault Judy if she took the easy path through life. She could make excuse after excuse and no one could find fault. But Judy has never allowed her disability to slow her momentum; in fact, she sees it as one of her greatest challenges, requiring her to dig deep for success and fulfillment. As someone with a weakened physical body, Judy has to excel mentally, emotionally, and spiritually to have the edge to achieve her ultimate visions for life.

Instead of taking the low road, Judy climbs vigilantly toward her vision daily. Her day starts by time set aside to recharge spiritually as she connects with God. The rest of her day, she pushes harder than anyone I know to attain excellence in everything from her appearance (she never goes out the door looking anything but her absolute best), to her daily contacts, to investing in those she supervises, to sharpening her next message, to reading and studying topics of interest to her personally and professionally.

Judy is a great picture for this section on sustaining momentum. Her mobility requires a manual wheelchair. It doesn't move unless she "pushes" it. If she pushes it a few times, it will coast a short distance on level ground and then begin to slow down until she pushes again. She tells the story of one road race in which the hill she encountered was so steep, she could only traverse it by zigzagging sideways slowly and arduously—pushing her weakened arm muscles to their absolute limits. If she had let up for one moment, she could have plummeted backwards down the hill to her death.

How hard are you pushing? Have you grown weary on your vision quest and find yourself hoping for enough momentum to coast the rest of the way home? Or are you attacking that vision of yours just as Judy attacked "Doomsday Hill"?

Momentum requires fuel … you must push with all your strength on every turn of those wheels to keep the forward fire. Judy could push like a quadriplegic, slowly plugging down the sidewalk. But she chooses to push like an Olympic athlete.

Are you pushing like a champion headed toward the most important finish of your life; or are you pushing like a person whose vision became disabled somewhere along the way? When you start to let up, think of Judy.

Here is what one of my life heroes and great friends, Joni Eareckson Tada, has to say about Judy Siegle: *"When disability struck Judy, she discovered some incredible life-changing keys to character development and peace of mind … showing us how to see the potential for change and possibility in our own crazy circumstances."*

There it is, one of the enemies of our journey toward vision—*crazy and out of control circumstances.* Most people allow themselves to be blindsided and thrown off course by unexpected events. Here is where the champions are divided from the quitters. The champion calls it resistance training, pressing harder toward the finish line. The quitter calls it tension, saying *"I can't take it. I quit here."*

Are you a champion or a quitter? Does your vision matter enough to push it forward as if it is of Olympic importance? I know the words my friend would leave with you as you consider how you will recharge and refine your vision. She would tell you with the most enthusiastic tone imaginable, *"The game may change, but the game goes on."* Today is your day to decide if the game will go on. You have come too far to not keep pushing, even if you are pushing uphill. And once you have pressed through, the view from the other side will leave you breathless as your vision completion comes into view.

Chapter Discoveries

- The most fulfilling professional successes are fueled by passion.

- Your passions will take you further than your skill set.

- You can actually fail your way to success.

- The degree of belief you place in yourself will determine the level of your potential.

- Failure holds the power to be one of our greatest training tools, teaching key strategies and lessons that no textbook or college course can offer.

- The most important step in recharging your vision is to make sure it is *your* vision.

- Having small achievable goals in place and tracking progress will build powerful momentum toward the bigger vision.

- Momentum must be recharged and refined to not lose power. There is no room for "auto pilot" in the life of the visionary.

Tension Points

- Creating goals and plans based upon your skill set while disregarding your passions

- Failing to connect your days to your deepest passions

- Misinterpreting performance and perfectionism for accomplishment

- Allowing past failures to dictate your destiny

- Failing to take essential breaks for recharging and refining vision and direction

- Entertaining momentum killers: procrastination, doubt, lack of vision

Activate Your Coaching Breakthrough

- Fuel your motivation by strengthening a passion. Do something you love this week.

- Re-define failure as part of your ultimate success: name one of your greatest failures. Now ask yourself, *"What did that failure teach me that will perfectly equip me for shaping and reaching my vision?"*

- Make an appointment with yourself to recharge and refine. Take a personal vision retreat.

- Identify one obstacle that keeps slowing your momentum, and get creative on how to eliminate or reduce its impact on your efforts.

Chapter 4
Ultimate Focus Required

"Motivation is what gets you started. Habit is what keeps you going."
–Jim Rohn

If you have ever had to re-evaluate, alter, or refine a goal somewhere along the way then you will be able to relate to another lesson I have learned in my hours logged flying small planes. Even though flying out the mid-portion of a flight—that place between takeoff and landing—can be mundane and arduous, it is not optional. *It is essential.*

If you are on the ground living out a vision, this section of your journey is where you are at highest risk for bailing out. *This is where most people give up and give in.*

Perhaps most would do well to imagine that, instead of flying out their visions, they are flying out a flight plan in a plane, because in the air, bailing out mid-flight is simply not an option. I have yet to meet a pilot whose long range vision is to crash.

For those who do not bail out, another tension point presents itself—the urge to lose focus and alertness. Once a vision is well underway, it is easy to back off and let up on the throttle. The visionary is hands-on as their vision is taking off, but auto pilot seems all too tempting once that vision seems to be off the ground.

As the pilot of any plane, small course corrections of only a few degrees at a time can determine whether you end up in New York or Chicago. Course corrections need to be made throughout the entire flight to stay on course. The same is true for your vision.

As a pilot, before the runway comes into view, you are flying blindly, dependent upon instruments, gauges, and feedback from the tower to determine your ultimate destination. As a person of vision, you are dependent upon your instincts, your desire, your commitment, and your support team to keep you headed in the direction of your dreams. Letting up for one moment can cause you to risk ending up far off course.

Goals and vision are much like gauges that the pilot must rely on. When practiced consistently, your goals become action steps which move you closer to your ultimate destination, daily.

When you set those goals that you initially believe will get you where you desire to be, you may realize along the way that some adjustments need to be made. Perhaps you fell behind last month and have to step it up this month to rebound. Perhaps your vision changes along the way, requiring a new path. Perhaps an unexpected life event causes you to have to take a short detour, such as a health challenge or a family member in crisis who needs you to travel across the country to care for them. Perhaps a change hits your industry, requiring powerful adjustments to stay in the game.

Whatever the case may be, you have to be in tune and alert enough to recognize when those slight goal adjustments must be made in order to steer you in the direction of your ultimate vision.

Again, one of my favorite concepts to teach is this: Practice does not make perfect. Perfect practice makes perfect. Doing the right things *consistently* are a sure guarantee for reaching your desired destinations.

The Power of Being Consistently Consistent

Definition of consistent: *reliable, steady, coherent and uniform, in agreement.*

Definition of persistent: *refusing to give up or let go; persevering obstinately; insistently repetitive or continuous; enduring.*

Consistency and persistence are secret weapons of the person who battles to hold onto their vision until it becomes reality.

In a recent meeting a business associate made a powerful statement. He said, *"The key to success is to be consistently consistent."*

That one statement sparked great interest. Then, I remembered something I had read years ago in one of my favorite books by Laurie Beth Jones called, *Teach Your Team to Fish.* In her book, Laurie investigates the significance of the number seven and draws the following conclusions:

"Seven means diligence. Seven means faith. Seven means perseverance. Seven means completion. Team builders need to ensure that team members do not give up on the third or fourth try.

In advertising, I learned that a person has to see your message an average of seven times before he or she gets it. I can't help wondering how our workplaces would change if we started to implement the rule of seven. We will contact a customer at least seven times in order to get our message across. We will realize that the seven customers we have are enough to build our company on. We will forgive each other at least seven times a day. We will attack this problem seven times if that is what it takes for the resistance to crumble."

When was the last time you quit on the third or fourth try? Are you ready to break through the tension point of lack of perseverance that paralyzes many? Aristotle said it well, *"We are what we repeatedly do. Excellence, then, is not an act, but a habit."*

Some of us start out on the right track, doing some of the right things most of the time. As time passes, we slip a bit and find ourselves doing some of the things less of the time. The next thing you know, we are not connecting the action of our days to our greater visions at all. Life comes at us fast. We have to battle against those urgent items that tug at our time and resources, pulling us off course, if we do not endure and continuously take repetitive, right actions.

Edward Barnes was a man who learned the power of being consistently consistent. Napoleon Hill shares his story in *The 17 Principles of Personal Achievement*:

"Edward C. Barnes was a man of much determination but few resources. He was determined to ally himself with the greatest mind of his day, Thomas Edison. When he arrived in Edison's office unannounced, his poor appearance made the clerks laugh, especially when he revealed that he had come to be Mr. Edison's partner. Edison had never had a partner. But his persistence got him an interview with Edison, and that interview got him a job as a handyman.

Edison was impressed with Barnes's determination, but that alone was insufficient to convince him to take the extraordinary step of making him a partner. Instead Barnes spent years cleaning and repairing equipment, until one day he heard Edison's sales force laughing over the latest invention, the Dictaphone.

They said it would never sell. Why replace a secretary with a machine? But Barnes, the handyman, jumped up and cried, "I can sell it!" He got the job.

For a month Barnes pounded the New York City pavement on a handyman's salary. At the end of that month he had sold seven machines. When he returned to Edison, full of ideas for selling more machines all across the country, Edison made him his partner in the Dictaphone business, the only partner Edison ever had."

What made Barnes so important to Edison? The inventor had thousands of people working for him, but only Barnes was willing to display his faith in Edison's work and put that faith into action. He didn't demand a fancy expense account and a big salary to do it, either.

Barnes focused favorable attention on himself by rendering service far beyond a handyman's responsibility. As the only one of Edison's employees to render this service, he was the only one who uncovered such tremendous benefits for himself.

Mr. Barnes accomplished that which seemed impossible. A couple of his strategies are worth taking note. First of all, it is clear that he had the confidence to believe he would realize his goal of making partner with Edison. The moment your confidence begins to falter, you are at risk of bailing out on your dream.

Next, we see a man who was willing to offer the work of a sales executive on the salary of a handyman. Those who complete powerful visions almost always share this trait in common: they realize sacrifices are required, so they expect them from the beginning, embrace them when they came along, and keep their eyes on the prize when it feels they were working harder than ever, for less return on their investment.

Mr. Barnes also displays another admirable and rare trait. He got his start by coming under someone great for training and experience, and he was willing to share the glory. Successful visionaries are often seen supporting other visionaries, enjoying the camaraderie and company of those like-minded individuals who simply cannot settle for status quo.

Finally, Mr. Barnes was consistent when others were giving up and even doubting him. My background is in sales. After training sales people for over a quarter of a century, I realized an interesting trend: the average salesman quits after the second "no." Yet most of the sales are made after the seventh "no." If you don't persist through some adversity, you're going to go broke as a salesman.

I realized something else. Many people will say "no" because they don't understand. Therefore, the sales executive must learn to hear a "no" as an opportunity to educate the potential client on the product or service being offered—persist, persist, persist. It will pay off.

Discipline Will be Required

In *Maximum Achievement*, Brian Tracy shares an old fable that emphasizes the power of disciplined action:

"Many years ago, in ancient Greece, a traveler met an old man on the road and asked him how to get to Mount Olympus. The old man, who happened to be Socrates, replied by saying, *'If you really want to go to Mount Olympus, just make sure that every step you take is in that direction.'* The moral of the story is simple, if you want to be successful and happy, just make sure that your every thought and action are taking you in that direction."

In this story, we see several key strategies found as common denominators in the lives of high achievers:

• Every thought lining up with the intended vision.

- Every action step being taken in the direction of the intended vision.

- A systematic, purposeful, consistent way of disciplining ones thoughts in keeping with the vision.

This way of thinking and living leaves no room for lack of confidence, doubt, second guessing, blame, procrastination, or holding grudges toward those who try to block your success. Take time today to weed out patterns of thinking and behaviors that do not move you in the direction of your intended vision.

For those of us who have worked in sales, we need to be reminded to keep our relationships with potential clients at the forefront of our vision for success. You have to be willing to do the hard work of investing in relationships which build trust and set you apart as the one they choose to do business with short term and long term. If you get greedy and too intent on making a sale, you will end up coming off as insincere and risk losing the sale. Ask questions and listen to what they need. Show genuine interest in their story and their needs. Strategically show them how you can commit to meet that need with your product or service. If you lose your sincerity and fail to care about the benefits to the client, it may be time for a new profession.

Before launching out into the business world, I

(Harold) was a state trooper. When I went into sales, I knew nothing about selling. I was given a script and told what to say and do. Needless to say, about five months into it, I had a nice collection of failures. Then I was introduced to a book that addressed closing sales, my weak link. In it, I discovered a chapter that talked about how you need to persist in your efforts to close a sale. That was the turning point. That's when I realized persistence and consistency must become a part of who I am—a part of my lifestyle.

My career began to turn around, because I had become consistent in my closing attempts. When I added persistence to the equation, I began making a lot of sales.

I think of John. John was a salesman whom I trained in selling. He quickly advanced, and went on to win salesman of the year four years in a row—beating me out his second year. When they asked his secret, he said, *"I do what Harold did, and I do it every day. I'm consistent in what he taught."* John was consistent in his efforts and he persisted until he got the job done. He had the discipline, the consistency, and the persistence just to go Step A, B, C … he would do it in order. It worked. His power was in his consistency and in his persistence. He could not have tapped into that power unless he had been willing to be coached. He enjoyed the power of being trainable and the rewards that followed.

I knew when I traveled on the road that I would make one sale out of every three presentations on average; however, during the week of my divorce, I made thirty-three presentations without a sale. I was down and discouraged. I desperately needed the money. So I got up the next morning determined to do what I knew to do—I remained consistent as I persisted in my efforts—and I made seven sales in a single day.

The only difference between that morning and the previous mornings was the fact that I made a phone call to Zig Ziglar's office before I went to work. I had taken some training courses—not by accident, but by God's divine intervention. I was connected to one of the trainers, and I shared what I was going through; he sat me down and talked to me for about fifteen or twenty minutes. His encouragement and wisdom helped to realign my attitude. Because I reached out and asked for help, it ended up being one of the best days I've ever had, on the heels of one of the worst weeks I've ever had. Amazing! Great opportunity and great reward await at those points where we are willing to reframe the impossible, and persist with consistency while others are quitting.

Remember my scenario of imagining being asked to land that commercial airliner? My decision to accept that challenge—my response in a time of crisis—had the power to affect hundreds, if not thousands of lives—not just my own life.

It is important to remember, as we seek to fuel our ultimate journeys toward success and achievement, that others will be affected if we bail out along the way. We said it before and it bears being said again: you have nothing to lose and everything to gain by going after your higher visions. Plus, others will also be impacted in a positive way by the best of your success.

> YOU HAVE NOTHING TO LOSE AND EVERYTHING TO GAIN BY GOING AFTER YOUR HIGHER VISIONS

Persistence is a dying art, right along with being consistent. How many individuals can you think of whose lives are defined by: refusing to give up or let go, perseverance, endurance, reliability, steady efforts? We live in a society driven by instant gratification. When people don't get the results they are looking for, they are off to the next thing. When a turn in an industry challenges profitability, many abandon that industry for the next hot business pursuit.

If you want to be on the cutting edge of success, learn to stick out the tough days while others are giving up and walking away. Many of today's great companies and organizations hung around and ended up with the market share that once belonged to yesterday's competitors who become today's quitters. There may come a time to bail out and cut losses if you are in an industry that takes a hard hit, but be patient, count the costs, and do your homework before walking away from something you have invested countless dollars and hours in. You may just be a short distance away from your ultimate destination coming into clear view.

I trained a gentleman a few years ago who had been downsized out of a crashing industry. As one of his first coaching assignments, I asked him to complete a skills and natural gifts assessment. He believed his industry could be re-invented and that he had valuable skills to contribute to its reshaping. He refused to believe that his product and services would become obsolete. He quickly went to work crafting an imaginary job description, one that would have the authority and the innovative power to turn a business around. He then took the initiative to market himself within the remaining companies serving this dying industry. One employer took the risk, hiring him on in a role he had designed himself. A few short years later, that company has risen to the top and attributes part of its success to his persistence and ingenuity. *That can be your story.*

Those with the power and the heart to stick out the "painful middle" section of any journey, seeing it through the challenges, are almost always surrounded by a great team. In fact, that team is not just there to fulfill your vision, but to be instrumental in shaping certain aspects of the journey as you give them opportunity to make valuable contributions and share in the successes along the way. Who you surround yourself with is so crucial to your ultimate success that we have chosen to conclude this chapter with a section devoted to building your support team well in advance.

In his bestselling book, *Good to Great,* Jim Collins offers a great piece of wisdom that sets apart good companies from truly great companies. This advice can be applied to your own business and team development:

> "When we began the research project, we expected to find that the first step in taking a company from good to great would be to set a new direction, a new vision and strategy for the company, and then to get people committed and aligned behind that new direction.
>
> We found something quite the opposite.
>
> The executives who ignited the transformations from good to great did not first figure out where to drive the bus and then get people to take it there. No, they first got the right people on the bus (and the wrong people off the bus) and then figured out where to drive it. They said, in essence, *'Look, I don't really know where we should take this bus. But I know this much: If we get the right people on the bus, and the wrong people off the bus, then we'll figure out how to take it someplace great.'"*

Sometimes vision is driven by who and what you have access to, coupled with your deepest desires. Having the right people in place will be a critical strategic move for anyone who intends to go the distance. Rubbing shoulders daily with those you respect and care for will be a key ingredient for keeping the passion for your unique vision alive on the hard dry days—helping you fly out the "painful middle."

Have Strategies in Place to Offset Obstacles and Challenges

"Start the applause even when it might appear that all possibilities are gone and that there is little or no hope."
–Maryanna Young

Obstacles and challenges are inevitable in life and business. If that is true, then why do some fall while others press forward and ultimately claim the prize of their vision?

The answer is simple: *some envision and prepare for challenges while others ignore the warning signs.* Strategic achievers plan while apathetic dreamers stand on the sidelines passively, creating a golden opportunity for an unexpected challenge to blindside them into giving up.

If you are reading this book, you are not among those who are passive. But you may be among the good company of those who do not know how to effectively offset harsh or unwanted circumstances. In which case, you are in need of a bit of inspiration.

In my first book (Kim), *Don't Miss Your Boat: Living With Purpose in the Real World,* my co-author Maryanna Young shared a powerful story that relates to overcoming obstacles. As an elite level athlete, coach, and agent, Maryanna has had more than her fair share of amazing encounters with amazing athletes. This story is no exception, as she shares her experience of watching the 10,000 meter race at the *NCAA Track and Field Championships* a few years back. This event serves to set many athletes up for the ultimate sporting achievement—one of the steps before the Olympic Trails and a shot at the Olympics.

As a former competitor herself, Maryanna realized the weight this event held for many of the runners. The 10,000 meter race is long and grueling, over twenty-five laps on the track. Many fans lose interest as laps blur together mid-race—imagine how it feels for the athletes.

As Maryanna shared this story, she highlighted that the stands were filled with well over twenty-thousand spectators. Let's pick up the story in her words:

"Just as the race began, a woman who was favored to win suddenly stepped to the side of the track and dropped to one knee. The crowd gasped and then groaned as they realized that this highly successful athlete had been stepped on by another athlete, causing her to lose her shoe. In the time it took her to replace her track shoe, the other runners had raced ahead of her, leaving her at least a quarter of a lap behind the pack.

People in the stands began to talk about how unfortunate it was for such a great competitor to be out of a critical race due to circumstances beyond her control. Most of the crowd obviously expected her to walk off the track and chalk up her fate in the race to a disastrous mishap. How many of us make that same mistake when our circumstances overwhelm us and life feels beyond our control? All too often, we abandon what we were destined for in life. We give in to the circumstances that surround us.

What happened next is a scene that I will never forget.

The twenty-one-year-old, 105 pound athlete leaped to her feet and began to get back on pace to finish her remaining twenty-five laps. By now, she was an enormous distance back from the pack of runners. As she got back in the rhythm of running, it seemed unlikely that she would even finish the race. If she did finish, it appeared that she would be left out of award contention. The fans muttered about how dismal it was that this young woman's hard work had been completely wasted, and would cause her to finish short of where her potential might have taken her.

Each lap, the fallen runner developed a faster rhythm to her stride. Miraculously, she was moving closer to the back of the pack of swiftly moving athletes. As a few more laps went by, it was clear that she was going to catch this group of the best collegiate runners in the world. As several more laps passed, the crowd moved their focus from the group of women leading the race. Nearly every eye was locked upon the wiry young runner as she came from the back of the pack, inching her way closer to the leaders. Every person I could see began rising to their feet and watching with amazement as this small, possibly injured athlete was making an unbelievable comeback.

As each lap passed, the cheering crowd was louder than at any *Super Bowl*. Each person there seemed to get louder and louder as they began to share the mission of this unbelievable woman who wouldn't give in to her impossible situation … With four laps to go, the woman with a dream in her heart, a vision in her mind and a crowd's deafening support was only fifteen steps behind the leaders. The fans sensed that she could not only make her way back to a respectable finish, but she now had the chance to win.

Leigh Daniel did the impossible that day. She came from 100 meters behind and won the *NCAA Championships* to the deafening roar of the crowd."

Doesn't that story make you feel as if you are in the crowd, on the edge of your seat, cheering for her victory? I have chosen to include this amazing comeback of Leigh's because it perfectly illustrates the power we have to overcome obstacles and challenges that stand in our way. As in Leigh's story, you need to position yourself to:

- Quickly diffuse challenges.

- Get back in the race with increased confidence.

- Gain rhythm and speed effectively.

- Pace to win.

- Listen for the encouragement.

- Rip the finish tape with your own chest.

- Never look back … what could have been your greatest tragedy might become your greatest victory and your finest hour.

We would like to offer these five key strategies that will empower you to overcome obstacles and get back on track effectively:

- Plan for the race.

- Train more than you think is enough.

• Learn to quickly diffuse challenges and get back in the race.

• Find your stride and pace yourself to win.

• Position yourself to take the most meaningful prize.

Train and Plan for the Race

In his *Performance Planner,* Mr. Ziglar lays out a simple system that has been a great tool for me over the years. First, he encourages the visionary to set goals and capture them in writing. Secondly, list the benefits that will be associated with achieving each goal. In the next critical step, list the possible obstacles and challenges that might be encountered. The final step is to draft a plan of action for achievement, including strategies for overcoming the obstacles.

An example would be a goal of losing weight. Let's say your obstacle is a love of sweets. Your plan of action is to only eat fruit snacks during the week and have a sweet treat one time each week, on a given day, as a reward. This is a simple example, but illustrates the simplicity of this system.

Another example: the goal of meeting with your coach or accountability partner weekly. The obstacle is procrastination. Your simple strategy includes making an appointment with yourself on your calendar for this week's session, marking it urgent, and prepaying your coach. You will be more likely to follow through if you have made a financial investment and learn to hold your commitments to your own development as sacred appointments.

Simply put, you must train and plan before you enter the race toward your vision. Training and planning for elite athletes involves running the race in their mind before it is run on the track. Mental exercises allow you to envision the course and the possible pitfalls that await.

Train More Than You Think is Enough

In 1973 I (Harold) resigned from the *Illinois State Police* and went into training to be a salesman. After a few short months of success, I was promoted to sales manager. I was excited, but concerned about the responsibility of helping others succeed. Because of that concern I became a student of training and management. Some of that training continues today, some thirty-eight years later, through books and courses.

My co-author, Kim, went back into training to receive foundational education from an accredited life coaching university just over a decade ago when she launched her coaching business. After a full decade of successfully coaching and training groups and individuals, she decided enough was not enough. She enrolled in a new college-level program in the effort to secure her current ranking that puts her in the elite minority, that of Master Coach. Kim and I have talked about our life long learning efforts and we both agree: in order to train and equip others, you must lead by example, continuing to train and equip yourself first.

Learn to Quickly Diffuse Challenges and Get Back in the Race

Leigh Daniel never lost focus, not even when another runner ripped her shoe right off in stride. She immediately dropped to one knee, fixed the problem, and got up running. If she had taken time to mentally analyze her next steps and to note how far she had fallen behind, she probably would have resigned to fail, and headed for the sideline. But she just did what she had trained to do … she ran—and to everyone's amazement, *she won!*

Leigh gives us a powerful lesson: *Never give your circumstances more power than they deserve.* Her lost shoe handicapped her, but it did not disqualify her. Imagine what would have happened if she had lost confidence for even a moment. Instead, she deflected the doubt and actually raised her confidence when circumstances tried to force her to lose confidence.

The next time a challenge comes your way, just do what you know to do. Keep moving forward relentlessly

… get back in the race! And try allowing that challenge to actually increase your confidence. You have survived some things in life, proving it can be done again. Don't get caught giving mental ascent to the limiting thoughts that exist to bring you down. Look up and look forward. Run, run, run!

LEIGH DANIEL WAS A CHAMPION IN HER OWN MIND LONG BEFORE SHE CROSSED THE FINISH LINE

Leigh Daniel was a champion in her own mind, just like my friend Judy Siegle, long before she crossed the finish line. She did not sit around for hours training for and envisioning losing her shoe. She trained for and envisioned taking the gold. So, when the shoe fell, she did all she had trained to do—she kept running to win. We must do the same if we are going to join the ranks of our champion level friends.

Find Your Stride and Pace to Win

Challenges can come at us fast and hard. Such was the case for Montel Williams when, at the height of his media career, he was diagnosed with multiple sclerosis. He has adopted a powerful mental tool that has allowed him to increase his speed, success, and vision while actually living with a disease that daily threatens to slow him down. He appears to be outrunning the enemy!

In *The Compound Effect,* Darren Hardy shares what he learned as he interviewed Montel:

"He told me about the strict diet he maintains because of the disease. Montel has adopted something called *'The Add-in Principle,'* and I think it's a wildly effective tool for anyone with any goal.

'It's not so much what you attempt to take out of your diet,' he explained to me, *'it's what you put in instead.'* This has become his analogy for life. Instead of thinking that he has to deprive himself, or take something out of his diet (e.g., *'I can't eat a hamburger, chocolate, or dairy'*), he thinks about what he can have instead (e.g., *'Today I'm going to have salad and steamed vegetables and fresh figs'*). He fills his focus and his belly with what he can have, so he no longer has attention or hunger for what he can't. Instead of focusing on what he has to sacrifice, Montel thinks about what he gets to 'add in.' The result is a lot more powerful."

Champion athletes make a lot of sacrifices, and anyone with a vision worth attaining will too. Before you enter the race, you must determine that it is worth the cost. Often the effect of unexpected obstacles, or just outright discovery that this journey is harder than imagined, can be enough to get the less committed individual to sit down and give up.

But the Montel Williams of this world would never settle for such low living. They face a challenge as resistance training, something that when pushed against, will increase their strength and endurance for the journey. This type of individual keeps a running account and reminder of the benefits, and how they outweigh the necessary sacrifices.

A few short years ago, on October 31st, Bethany Hamilton lost her left arm in a vicious shark attack while sharpening her surfing skills off the coast of Kauai, in hopes of attaining status as a professional female surfer. Less than a month after she almost bled to death en route to emergency surgery, she surfed again. Less than a year later, this one-armed fighting bandit took on her fellow two-armed surfing competitors, and joined the ranks as a professional with no adaptations or special concessions.

She pushed and paddled her way back with one arm and a heart filled with determination to take hold of her vision. I love what she says in her book and in the movie, *Soul Surfer: "I don't need easy. I just need possible."*

Surfing was not on her resume. Surfing was in her soul. If your vision is limited to what you hope to see one day on your resume to make you more profitable, more marketable, or more proud, you have missed the mark. Challenges will likely cause you to abandon a limited vision mid-way into the race. But if your current vision is anchored in your soul, you will run, surf, and fight your way to the finish, because a true visionary refuses to die or quit.

A true visionary will run with a damaged shoe, run with wheels in place of legs, or surf without an arm, if that's what it takes. You may cross the finish line a bit bruised and disfigured by the challenges of the race. But those scars can become the honorable marks of one who refused to lie down and give up. It has been medically proven that a bone heals stronger than it was before (when there are no complications to the healing process). Your scars should not be your embarrassment—they should be your badges of honor for crossing the finish line to the roar of those who once thought your win was absolutely impossible!

Position Yourself to Take the Most Meaningful Prize

You've got to run in the right race to attain the prize you are envisioning. Visions are specific. We are not all Olympic runners or professional surfers. But we all want the chance to fulfill our potential.

Positioning yourself for success first requires reassessing and making absolutely sure that the race you are entering (the vision in your heart) is the one that means the most to you. Make sure the race you are running is birthed in your own spirit.

The next key element in positioning yourself for success is to stay in contact with your "tower." If we could talk to Leigh Daniel as we discuss her story, I wonder how much weight she would put on the cheers that started small and grew into a thunderous wave? How much of a difference did that encouragement make as she crossed the finish line, breaking that tape with her own chest?

Your tower—your own fans in the stand—are crucial. They keep the cheers coming, even when you drop behind. I have never forgotten advice given to me as I (Kim) left the security of a high paying job to start my venture as a Life Coach and Speaker. A friend reminded me to *"never surrender my vision to negative thinking people."* Fill your stands with those who will cheer you on and who will run alongside of you in your race toward your vision. Remember the key rule of the person in need of encouragement. Choose to be an encourager, giving away freely that which you so desperately need.

Pilots are taught to look ahead. Before the runway comes into view, storms, clouds, oncoming air traffic, mechanical issues, control malfunctions all threaten to impact the flight plan. As a result, the pilot trains in strategies to implement if and when such challenges occur. The wise visionary also trains and prepares for obstacles, while refusing to give them undue weight. They are what they are: obstacles were meant to be flown over, under, or around; the most confident of pilots fly right through the heart of a storm. The ride might get a bit bumpy, but you will fly it out as long as you keep your hand on the controls and your eye on the ultimate landing.

Break the Tape With Your Own Chest

Herein exists the greatest benefit that will ever come to those who press through the tension, refusing to let go of their dreams and visions: *the thrilling exhilaration of breaking the tape with their own chest.*

I have shared some of my journey, and that my hardest lessons have come as I had to face the fact that some of my dreams were rooted in motives that failed to be fulfilling, such as increasing income which required less freedom and less down time. My journey and successes have proven most fulfilling when they gifted me with more of what I really long for: more freedom, more flexibility, more time to do what has become most important to me.

Making a good living is fine and well, as long as it does not keep you from making a great life for yourself, your family, and your friends. If it robs you of the most important things, it becomes a burden rather than a vision, and life begins to feel as if you are pressing toward the finish line wearing heavy shackles.

Give Yourself Permission to Move the Dates

Some finish lines can wait. Last year I (Harold) was running along when my mother passed away suddenly. I took off a couple of weeks, giving myself permission to grieve and to remember.

When I stepped back in the game, I had to step up the pace a little to make up for the time away. It took a while to regain my stride and my rhythm, and I purposed to be kind to myself and make extra allowances for the days when I did not feel quite up to par. All of my finish lines are still intact, and most of them can wait.

A key strategy is giving yourself some extra space and refusing to lose heart when an unexpected event makes a sneak attack, requiring your time and attention. These days, I actually feel as if I am honoring my precious mom as I keep the pace. I am pretty sure I can hear her voice cheering me on in the crowd.

We opened this chapter with a powerful idea inspired by the story of the amazing comeback of Leigh Daniels: *"Start the applause even when it might appear that all possibilities are gone and there is little or no hope."*

Are you living as if you fully expect to claim the prize regardless of what your current circumstances seem to be saying; or have you resigned any part of your mind to the possibility of failure? If you give doubt a chance, it will take you miles and miles off course. *Refuse to quit.*

Press on when the race is slanted against you. Determine and declare today that you will finish that which you have begun.

Your ultimate achievement is to be determined to envision crossing the finish line, even when your highest aim seems to be sabotaged by your current challenge. Remember, you already know what the doubting crowd did not know until many laps into that race: *You are destined to win and to claim your gold.* Now is your time and this is your race. Nothing or no one has the power to stop you—*except for you!*

Invest in Your Support Team
Before You Need Them

"None of us is as smart as all of us." –Ken Blanchard

The absolute first step in building your support team that will empower you to drive your visions to completion is this: *Determine to be coachable.* If you are not there, you are not ready to take this critical step. Take time to deal with any past issues that have caused you to build up a destructive resistance to positive feedback. Pride and arrogance need to take a hard hit at this step in the process. I am convinced that one of the most impermeable tension points ever encountered is a non-teachable spirit. For the rare few individuals who possess enough wisdom and initiative to fly solo and actually succeed, there remains one key problem. They are alone at the end of the journey. For me, half of the celebration of any victory is having people I love there to celebrate with me. Great leaders shoulder their portion of the blame and selflessly share the victory that belongs to them.

Know Where to Find the Answers

Napoleon Hill shares a high-impact story in *Think and Grow Rich* that perfectly highlights the importance of your support team. He calls this story, *The "Ignorant" Man Who Made a Fortune:*

"During the first World War, a Chicago newspaper published certain editorials in which, among other statements, Henry Ford was called, *'an ignorant pacifist.'* Mr. Ford objected to the statements, and brought suit against the paper for libeling him. When the suit was tried in the courts, the attorneys for the paper pleaded justification, and placed Mr. Ford, himself, on the witness stand, for the purpose of providing to the jury that he was ignorant. The attorneys asked Mr. Ford a great variety of questions, all of them intended to prove, by his own evidence that, while he might possess considerable specialized knowledge pertaining to the manufacture of automobiles, he was, in the main, ignorant.

Mr. Ford was plied with such questions as the following:

'Who was Benedict Arnold?' and *'How many soldiers did the British send over to America to put down the Rebellion of 1776?'* In answer to the last question, Mr. Ford replied, *'I do not know the exact number of soldiers the British sent over, but I have heard that it was a considerably larger number than ever went back.'*

Finally, Mr. Ford became tired of this line of questioning, and in reply to a particularly offensive question, he leaned over, pointed his finger at the lawyer who had asked the question and said, *'If I should really want to answer the foolish question you have just asked, or any of the other questions you have been asking me, let me remind you that I have a row of electric push-buttons on my desk, and by pushing the right button, I can summon to my aid men who can answer any question I desire to ask concerning the business to which I am devoting most of my efforts. Now, will you kindly tell me, why I should clutter up my mind with general knowledge, for the purpose of being able to answer questions, when I have men around me who can supply any knowledge I require?'*

There certainly was good logic to that reply.

That answer floored the lawyer. Every person in the courtroom realized it was the answer, not of an ignorant man, but a man of education. Any man is educated who knows where to get knowledge when he needs it, and how to organize that knowledge into definite plan of action. Through the assistance of his 'Mastermind' group, Henry Ford had at his command all the specialized knowledge he needed to enable him to become one of the wealthiest men in America. It was not essential that he have this knowledge in his own mind."

Develop Relationships for all the Right Reasons

After you have determined to be coachable, the next step in identifying the right support is humbly admitting that you will accomplish more while linked to great people (along with their network and resources) than you will on your own. I am always encouraged and expectant of a person's ultimate achievements when I see that they recognize this powerful truth: you are the sum of those with whom you choose to associate.

It is important to also create support relationships long before you actually need them. This allows relationships to develop out of mutual respect and the shared benefits of networking that can be highly mutual. If you wait to seek help right when you need it most, you risk coming across to others as the type of person who only seeks out others when you have something to gain. So go ahead. Identify some great supports and begin selflessly investing in them today. This will ensure you that a great pool of wisdom awaits when challenges come your way.

I would encourage you to create a simple strategy for finding and securing the right support needed to move you from dreamer to actual achiever. Perhaps this short list of suggestions will inspire your search; be on the lookout for supports in the form of:

- **Current Mentors:** Who is already in place in your life and business that you respect and look up to?

- **Local Icons of Success:** Who do you know in your own community or company that is already on the cutting edge of all you hope to accomplish? Invite them out for coffee and interview them, searching for their keys to success.

- **Social Networking:** The internet has opened up communication with national and international leaders. Many have joined communities such as Facebook and LinkedIn, and are willing to share their expertise.

- **Programs Offered by Your Company:** Many companies and industries have associations, conferences, and training opportunities that you can take advantage of.

- **Technology and Internet:** Make sure you are equipped with the technology that can make success easier for you. Many computer and technology companies offer student discounts to those studying a certain field. Use Google and the many other search engines to find free resources for your area of desired development. The internet has become the world's largest and easiest mall to access.

- **Be Industry Specific:** Many industries offer leads for purchase that are specific to your business goals. Try searching the internet again, and don't forget to begin with key websites of your company and your industry.

- **Expand Your Wisdom:** Find industries with a critical link to your own business and consider expanding your knowledge base to include their strategies and systems. For example, a counselor might benefit from expanding their learning into the world of life coaching. Another example might be a company CEO benefitting from taking a communications course.

- **Community College:** One of the great overlooked resources might be in your own back yard. Your local community college offers many courses at bargain prices that could directly or indirectly benefit you in achieving your goals. A tip here is that most continuing education programs are free to senior citizens who are staying in the game of life aggressively.

- **Use What You Already Know:** Before you set out to gain new knowledge bases, make sure you are consistently putting into practice what you already know. Most people I have worked with and trained over the years have a wealth of personal development materials collecting dust on the book shelves in their offices. *Don't get overwhelmed here.* Simply go over to that shelf and choose one that really spoke to you in the past and revisit it in the coming weeks.

You've got to be honest with where you are—you may not be in the pilot's seat, but you are in the driver's seat of your own life and business vision. The pilot in need of instruction is going to call on the pilot with more experience and greater talent than he possesses. Gain access and begin associating on a regular basis with those who are ahead of you in your area of influence. Learning from the best is one of the shortest paths to becoming your personal best.

Theodore Roethke once said, *"What we need is more people who specialize in the impossible."* This implies the power in becoming someone who specializes in what was formerly considered impossible. The cutting edge visionary will take that truth one step further, and surround himself with those who also specialize in the impossible. If you are going to do the hard work of recruiting and securing a solid support team, make sure you go after individuals whom you have to run to keep up with.

Refuse to let the tension points of insecurity and pride stand in the way of your success. Press through and you will find that your network really does increase your net worth.

Also, make sure you avoid another key mistake. Far too many people engage their supports in the beginning of their journey toward success, only to pass them off along the way, feeling that they are no longer needed. Stay on the cutting-edge by staying connected to your tower throughout your entire journey. Those who hold a high and objective view of where you are headed can warn you of oncoming traffic, pending dangers, upcoming storms, and the landing strip that you were about to fly right over in the fog.

Who do you need in your tower? Evaluate where you are headed and what will be needed for your success. Some supports may include: life and business coaches, consultants, technology consultants, financial experts, business attorneys, marketing specialists, and accountability partners. Then remember; never abandon your support tower mid-journey. You will need them along the way, and your flight to your ultimate destination will be safer, smoother, and quicker with the right people in place.

CHAPTER DISCOVERIES

- Those who refuse to bail out are uniquely positioned to inherit opportunities thrown away by those who quit prematurely.

- Many bail out because they fail to revisit the benefits of their ultimate vision, leaving them short sighted and quick to bail out when challenges come.

- Consistency and persistence turn dreamers into achievers.

- Take a proactive approach to challenges and obstacles by setting strategies in place to diffuse them when they occur.

- You are the sum of those with whom you choose to associate. Raise the bar and select your team wisely.

- Recognize the value of your support relationships by investing in them unconditionally.

TENSION POINTS

- Giving up just before success comes

- Failing to be persistent and consistent

- Being blindsided by obstacles and challenges ... spending too much time hoping you will avoid them and not enough time planning for how to offset them

- Being paralyzed by discouragement

- Failing to build key support relationships before needing them

- Viewing support relationships as a one-way street, not recognizing your responsibility to mutually invest in those who support you

- Allowing intimidation to keep you from interacting with and recruiting high achievers onto your team of support

ACTIVATE YOUR COACHING BREAKTHROUGH

- Name one strategy that has brought you success that you have failed to practice consistently. Start implementing that strategy into every day.

- Identify potential obstacles and challenges and create a pro-active strategy to offset their impact. Learning the art of prevention saves time and energy.

- Infuse your life with encouragement by seeking ways to be an encourager to those around you.

• Taking a look at your greatest visions, what will be required to succeed? What supports will you need in place? Identify one high priority team member and make plans to invest in and connect with them this week.

CHAPTER 5
Live and Lead with Vision

"A key part of the life of vision is owning the responsibility of seeing others embrace this wonderful adventure."
                                                        –Kim Fletcher

We live by example. Our own lives easily point to that which is of utmost importance to us.

Vision-keepers see other people. While professional pursuits always will be competitive, there are ruthless competitors and there are compassionate competitors.

I would rather be kind than right every time. I would rather take great people with me on my journey toward my ultimate dreams than go it alone. I long for my gains and successes to create a life brimming over with resources and influence that can be used to bless, encourage, and impact others so they can embrace the same potential for success that has been entrusted to me.

I (Kim) spent nearly twenty years as a physical therapist, navigating the health care industry before launching my life coaching and speaking business. I have been impacted by a stark contrast. In the health care arena, professionals were highly competitive and often hesitant to share their knowledge base. Perhaps it was fear of losing referrals that drove the secrecy. In the coaching industry, I have been amazed! Almost everyone is willing to selflessly share of their wisdom and resources freely. Ideas, referrals, and tips are shared with ease and without hesitation. *It has been a refreshing change of pace.*

How are you positioned? Are you willing to pass along the keys that you have gained through your own personal and professional experience? That is a mark of a truly selfless visionary, and we see a great example as told by Zig Ziglar in *See You at the Top:*

"An old man sat in a cathedral playing the organ. It was the end of the day and the setting sun shining through the beautiful stained-glass windows gave the old man an angelic appearance. He was a skilled organist playing sad and melancholy songs because he was being replaced by a younger man. At dusk, the young man rather brusquely stepped in the back door of the cathedral. As the old man noted his entrance, he removed the key from the organ, put it in his pocket, and slowly made his way to the back of the cathedral.

As the old man drew abreast of him, the young man extended his hand and said, 'Please, the key.' The old man took the key out of his pocket and gave it to the young man, who hurriedly walked to the organ. He paused for a brief moment, sat down on the bench, inserted the key, and started to play.

The old man had played beautifully and skillfully, but the young man played with sheer genius. Music such as the world had never heard came from the organ. It filled the cathedral, the town, and even the countryside. This was the world's first exposure to the music of Johann Sebastian Bach. The old man, with tears streaming down his cheeks, said, 'Suppose, just suppose, I had not given the master the key.'

It's obvious the old man did give the young man the key. It's also obvious the young man made full use of that key. It's a sobering thought, because we hold the key to the future of others. We don't live alone. Our actions and deeds affect other people, many of whom we will never know. That's the reason our obligation and responsibility for doing the best we can with what we have goes beyond our own personal lives."

For me, there is great joy in knowing that I might impart wisdom to someone else who ends up surpassing me as I move toward my vision. I love the idea that I can take the experience and wisdom I have gained in several decades of life and be able to accelerate someone else's journey.

Here is a revolutionary thought: *the greatest gift I can give someone is the opportunity to start, not where I started, but where I am today.*

If we start to fear the competition and find ourselves unwilling to be mentors, out of the hesitation that we want to be the best, we have just ceased to be our best and have set ourselves up for a devastating fall. Be willing to relinquish the position of "best" and hold fast to the position that is best for you.

I (Harold) wasn't threatened when John passed me in sales success. I was honored that I had something to do with his success. Determine today to press past your tension points of insecurity, fear, and self-focus. Proceed with boldness and confidence as you position yourself to live a life of vision, knowing that a key part of the life of vision is owning the responsibility of seeing others embrace this wonderful adventure.

Live from Vision to Vision

If we check in with the tower to see what they see, we would realize that, while we may be focused on our current flight plan (our current vision), they are overseeing a massive amount of activity in the air. From their perspective, there are numerous flight plans in motion simultaneously. It is their responsibility to give navigational feedback that allows ongoing flight plans to fly in the same airspace without anyone crashing into anything. *Quite a responsibility!*

When flying out one flight plan, or living out a specific vision that affects a key area of life, it is easy to forget what the tower sees clearly. Life is not made up of only one flight plan. The person of vision is simultaneously living out numerous visions at once; as one comes near completion, they do as any seasoned pilot—*they log another flight plan.*

This is what we mean by living from vision to vision. Recognize today that no one vision is large enough to last a lifetime or be fulfilling for all of life. You will likely juggle many successful visions at once, while repeating this pattern many times over the span of your life.

Be careful to avoid placing undue weight on one vision alone. We spoke of life balance earlier and we reiterate that key issue here. The person who focuses on business success alone, without considering how his or her personal life will be affected, is living shortsighted. True vision considers all aspects of life; it takes into account how one pursuit will affect every other aspect of life including wellness/health, relationships, free time, ability to contribute back to society, identity, and faith.

Take the key areas of life and craft simultaneous

visions (futuristic pictures) for each area. When considering launching a new vision, put it to the test by asking how it will affect the other key areas of your life. The benefits of a lasting vision will bring positive impact to every area of your life when that vision is well crafted.

To avoid disappointment and a sense of letdown, get your next flight plan ready to file as another flight comes to a close. This will keep you moving forward from vision to vision and will keep you motivated for life.

Refuse to Hit the Autopilot Switch

Success has a built-in risk. The moment you begin to feel successful, the tendency kicks in to move from full throttle effort to coasting. If we stick with our pilot picture, this risk would be going on "autopilot." Coasting only occurs in one direction … *downward!*

Vision to vision is critical. How many people work for retirement—only to die a year and a half later because they had nothing planned? When you reach your one goal in life, you should not proclaim that you are finished. I (Harold) could have retired at age sixty-five, but I realized that I would rather keep pressing forward. I wasn't finished as I found myself hungry for accomplishing more and mentoring others. My days

VISION TO VISION IS CRITICAL.

are filled with excitement. I am always planning another long-distance motorcycle ride, always on the lookout for someone else who is hungry to learn and to accomplish. That is what keeps me living from vision to vision. *What will keep you connected to this life of ongoing vision?*

> WHAT WILL KEEP YOU CONNECTED TO THIS LIFE OF ONGOING VISION?

My former boss, Jerry Gibson, went from being a factory worker to an extremely successful businessman. He was my role model then and he still is today. He taught me more than anybody else on earth. He graduated from the school of hard knocks but went from working in a factory to starting a program from his kitchen table. Once successful, he started another program. Once that was successful, some partners came in, and he started another program.

When I got involved, his first program was at risk of going by the wayside—I was asked to revive it. Suddenly, he had three things going on at one time. Three flight plans were being flown simultaneously. He went from being broke to being extremely successful. His success started with a vision. His program began in one town, but his vision included expanding to at least three states. His life is a great example of what it looks like to live vision to vision.

Try Something New

Mitchell Tolle is a great example of someone who is never afraid to try new things. He moves fast, always looking for a new business idea. Just a few short years ago, Mitchell was run down and broke by his own estimation.

Many years ago, with a vision of becoming a worldclass artist, he sold paintings of wildcats at a special price to grow awareness of his artistic talent—then the *Kentucky Wildcats* basketball team made it to the *Final Four*. He saw an opportunity and he took it.

Some years later, he expanded his business to include motivational speaking. Speaking professionally all across the nation ignited a deeper fire, the desire to preach the Gospel. That desire brings him to the present day where he leads a large church in Lexington, Kentucky.

It wasn't too many years ago when this starving artist was saying, *"I had hundreds of paintings in my building and nobody would buy them. I thought about having a bonfire … [but] I had that vision of becoming a world-class American artist. I kept that vision. I attained that goal."*

Today, Mitchell is known world-wide for his artistic ability—he is considered one of America's leading artists, a level of recognition and success that typically only come after an artist has passed on. Mitchell is living from vision to vision and he is enjoying great success as he lives. I can only imagine what flight plan he will file next.

Keep Your Bucket Full

I once met a man named John Godard. In his early days, he wrote down a hundred and twenty-seven goals that he hoped to accomplish by the end of his life. When we met, he was well into his seventies and excited that he still had ten or eleven of those goals he planned to reach.

We can learn a key from John. If you want to remain motivated, you need to have more goals and visions than you seem to have time or energy to reach. As they say, your grasp should always be farther than your reach.

When Donna and I first got married, I started telling her about all the different things I wanted to do. *"What do you think of all that?"* I asked. *"Hon,"* she said, *"you've got a lot of things you want to do."* I am not sure if she was impressed or overwhelmed. All I know is this: it is an exciting way to live, full of vision.

I keep an "idea book" where I take time daily to jot notes and review my ideas. This book includes creative ideas on how to attain certain goals, along with strategies for success.

The lifestyle of vision keeps me youthful and I believe it will be the same for you. I have met people in their fifties who seem old and people well into their eighties and nineties who are youthful and full of life. Staying motivated by a heart full of vision and passion is a sure path toward remaining young. Just as exercising your body helps to keep it fit and defy the years, exercising your heart through a life of vision keeps you emotionally, mentally, and spiritually young.

The visionary never fails to remember, as long as there is breath, your best days and greatest accomplishments lie ahead of you, not behind you. This visionary man or woman is never content with yesterday's achievement … vision looks forward, far and beyond what most would ever deem possible.

Become a Visionary Leader

"You teach what you know, but you reproduce who you are." –Zig Ziglar

In the last section, we began to touch on the importance of visionaries who are willing to pay their lifestyle forward so others can tap into and ultimately reach their full potential. To expand those thoughts in one simple phrase, *the visionary is uniquely equipped to lead!*

One of the most powerful ways to succeed is to begin duplicating yourself. That one simple practice can increase your impact and influence. The best of leaders live to reproduce themselves by empowering a new generation of leaders equipped to take current success to a whole new level.

> **THE WORLD HAS GROWN WEARY OF SELF-FOCUSED LEADERS WHO ARE POWER HUNGRY.**

We are in need of a fresh kind of leader. The world has grown weary of self-focused leaders who are power hungry. In much of my (Kim) group coaching and speaking over the past decade, I have come to appreciate some of the following traits in leaders of great influence. The high-integrity visionary leader prefers:

- **Mentoring rather than barking orders.** Take time today to ask yourself who you can bring along for the journey. Name one person whose entire life could be changed if you chose to invest in him. Make it a high priority to mentor others with the gifts and successes which have been entrusted to you.

- **Duplicating themselves selflessly rather than jockeying to stay in control.** Determine to find others who can join your vision in ways that create great partnership opportunities for them while increasing your effectiveness and impact. After ten years of working alone, I (Kim) expanded my solo enterprise to include associate coaches

LIVE AND LEAD WITH VISION

and speakers. The result has been an amazing team that I get to link arms with while we serve a wider variety and a larger number of clients with excellence. My work load reduced while my impact increased. I take more vacations than ever … *now that is a great deal!*

- **Leading by influence versus lording authority over others.** You can dictate to others from a distance if you are content to lead with authority and a heavy hand, but you will never be a true leader. A true leader inspires others to follow by choice, *not out of obligation.* Determine to be the kind of leader who influences others to want to follow the path you are paving. You will find the number of individuals growing behind you and backing you up increasing exponentially!

- **Being effective over being noisy.** Some so-called leaders like to hear themselves talk, constantly giving orders and micromanaging. The effective leader leads by example, not by incessant talking. Set your mind today that if your example is all your team had to follow, it would take your visions to the top. The quiet and effective leader doesn't have to say much. When that person shows up, the team is close at hand to learn and to follow.

- **Empowering over oppressing.** The seasoned and mature leader hates oppression. In fact, a key mark of the leader I would follow is someone who is the champion of people whom society has labeled as less valuable. Choose to put yourself ahead in the pack of leaders by becoming a champion of the downcast … replace any oppressive, arrogant behavior patterns with encouraging empowerment. If your team does not feel appreciated and respected, they will fail to show you what they know. They will never fulfill their potential under your watch. But if they know you are investing in them, your next greatest accomplishment might be sitting right next to you if you are willing to share the glory.

- **Being in tune rather than distant.** Get to know those around you. Tap into their true potential. Ask what they are passionate about. Most teams fail because they have the right people in the wrong roles. Take all you learned as we discussed identity and natural gifting, use it to re-evaluate who you have in position, and if the role they fill on your team is the best fit. You will unleash a new wave of ambition and accomplishment by empowering others to serve where they are gifted and passionate.

One of my favorite authors, Erwin Raphael McManus, describes the leader of influence in *Seizing Your Divine Moment:*

> "If you want to increase your influence, risk bringing people up close. Of course, it is important to first ask yourself the question, '*if I bring someone up close to see the real me, what will he see? Who will he become?'* The ultimate end and most profound result of influence is when a person is free from any command or power you may exert, and yet still reflects the influence of your values and passions … that is the challenge that is set before us—that we not only take initiative, that we not only move with confidence into the reality of uncertainty, but also that we maximize our sphere of influence as we grow in the depth of character."

This unique type of leader has one grand vision in mind—to take all of his or her current success and use it to accelerate the path for others who are interested in living a life of great vision.

Here is one final question that must be asked: *Will you choose to go it alone, causing your vision to die with you? Or will you choose the bravehearted path of the visionary leader who determines to take as many people as possible with him into the clearing of great success?* Today is the day to abandon any notion you may have held for going it alone, so all of the success will belong to you. That is a sure path to all of the heartache, stress, and disappointment belonging to you. Instead, choose the path of shared challenges and expanded joys; it will prove to be the adventure of a lifetime.

Lead by linking up with co-visionaries, reproduce yourself in others, and watch your vision explode exponentially into a grand display of impact and achievement. Then, get ready to have people you value—whom you have linked your life to—in position for the celebration that awaits. After all, *who wants to party alone?*

TIME FOR CELEBRATION!

At the heart of celebration is what you value. The amount of value which you ascribe to certain aspects of your vision journey will reflect whether or not you take time to celebrate, how you celebrate, how often you celebrate, and with whom you choose to celebrate. It will also affect whether you wait for a big accomplishment before you schedule the "party" or if you choose to celebrate throughout your vision quest.

This is not a chapter where the serious pursuit of vision gives way to careless play. Celebration is a key ingredient throughout the entire journey of the fully committed visionary. Show me the patterns of a person around this one topic, and I can almost predict their success potential and their degree of fulfillment.

In *Fresh Start,* Doug Fields shares a story that captured our nation:

"On September 18, 2007, computer science professor Randy Pausch stepped in front of an audience of four hundred people at Carnegie Mellon University to deliver a lecture titled *'Really Achieving Your Childhood Dreams.'* The talk was modeled after an ongoing series of lectures in which top academics are asked to ponder what matters most, and then give a hypothetical 'final talk' (e.g., What wisdom would you try to impart to the world if you knew it was your last chance?).

What was different about Pausch's last lecture was that the clock was truly ticking rapidly for him. With slides of his CT scans beaming out to the audience, Randy told his audience about the cancer that was devouring his pancreas and that would ultimately claim his life in a matter of months. An ironic image, perhaps, of someone who seemed so invincible but was so near the end of his time on earth."

Doug Fields goes on to share that the key question presented in Randy's lecture that day was simply, *"What do you value most?"*

Returning to our topic of celebration, what do *you* value most? We will certainly celebrate that which we value. With that in mind, *when was the last time you stopped to celebrate a significant milestone or achievement? Was it yours or someone else's?* You can quickly think of a graduation party or a birthday party you have attended (or that you failed to attend because of a full schedule). But, can you think of a time when you created a special occasion off the beaten path to really honor something that you or a loved one had accomplished?

In Hawaiian culture, history shows that in the early years of that culture's development, many challenges threatened the health and wellbeing of newborn babies. Many of those children did not live to see their first birthday. As a result, it became a cultural norm to celebrate the first birthday by going all out in celebration. Life held great value and their celebrations marked a key milestone.

Today, many years later, with improved healthcare and living conditions, babies easily make the one year mark. But a tradition of valuing life took hold and still shapes that culture today. With much aloha and lots of panache, a child's first birthday party in Hawaii is really something to behold—hundreds will attend the all day beach side parties, laughing, and enjoying the gift of life. Most of them probably called in for a day off work in order to show up!

Our point is simple … *you will celebrate what you value.* We need to evaluate if we have gotten too busy, too financially conservative, or too "grown up" to play.

We need a shift of perspective when we lose sight of the many blessings we have that warrant our full celebration. I heard excerpts of Pausch's last lecture, in which he honestly revealed how much he wished he could gain just a bit more time for what he truly valued most. If we would embrace the powerful messages left behind for us, we could live regret-free.

An eye-opening test of what we value comes in this assessment: *if you do take time to celebrate, do you wait until a big achievement, or are you on the cutting edge with those of us in the "celebration minority" who celebrate potential and hopes as they develop?* Waiting for the big accomplishment, before going after the reward, indicates a high value placed on performance. Celebration that occurs prematurely indicates a high value placed on the process, the vision, and the hope being held out for its completion; this method celebrates the person doing the accomplishing. I think both are essential, but I have to admit, I love celebrating the person *"just because."*

Many of us grew up in models of families where you would be rewarded or punished related to accomplishments (e.g., good grades or bad grades), but for most of us, the concept of being rewarded because we are alive and full of potential was absent from our upbringing. We learn early on in our culture that we have to achieve to be acknowledged and seen. In reality, we were born needing to be seen long before we had ever met a single goal. In the rare family system of being honored and rewarded for your life and potential, children grow into stable and peaceful individuals who go on to accomplish much out of a strong identity. Those raised in families which rewarded, or punished, performance often grow up insecure—under pressure, with a lifelong feeling that what they're doing is never quite enough.

Today is your day to begin (or increase) your efforts of celebrating life and potential, in yourself and in the lives of those you love. You don't have to schedule an expensive trip. I love books and often reward myself with a new purchase when reaching a goal. I also love a great ride on my Harley on a clear day. I take short rides when I need a boost; I schedule long trips to mark big achievements. Tomorrow, I am turning in this manuscript for its final edit and heading for Nova Scotia, while Kim is probably planning her next jaunt to her favorite island, Maui, Hawaii. My reward is a day on the bike. Hers is a day at her favorite secluded beach, sketch pad in hand.

Looking back, I realize that my most productive seasons of life have included more days off, more time to reflect, and more celebrations. In fact, one year I took six weeks of vacation and that proved to be my most profitable year to date. Of course, Kim beat me out with thirteen weeks as her all-time high; that was the year she launched her own business and gained the creative insights to make it happen.

Choose rewards that are meaningful to you and which do not create financial stress, which can be counterproductive. You may not be the crowd type or the beach type or the bike type—a great reward might be a solo backpacking trip, dinner for two, or a retreat with a few friends to a favorite getaway. Get creative and think up ten great rewards that are free. Here are a few ideas to get you thinking: schedule time to watch the sunset, enjoy a simple picnic, hike a beautiful ridge, indulge in a homemade frozen drink, teach a child to fly a kite, write a poem.

Fill your days and weeks with simple rewards—your favorite espresso, time for a swim, a new tennis racquet, time to sit alone and write in your journal.

Whatever you choose, do it often, make it personal, and bring along those who have encouraged you, invested in you, and made your successes possible.

Celebration honors life and potential while also marking great achievements. Yet, there is another powerful impact of living a life with an intentional focus on celebrating … *restoration!*

My (Kim) father has logged many hours restoring antiques. The word "restoration" is defined as: *the act of restoring, renewing, reviving, or reestablishing; repairing to the original condition.* Just as an antique armoire or a vintage wooden boat bears some scars with use, life is much the same. Challenges, periods of pressure and high demands, and the unending nature of it all leaves us chipped, nicked, dented, faded, and a bit rusty. Our bodies, our minds, our spirits, and our visions need times of restoration.

To restore a vintage boat requires taking it into the shop. It comes out of the water (its place of work) and enters a new environment where the sole purpose is its restoration. We need to take ourselves out of production on a regular basis for times that are about restoration, and restoration only.

As with many of our concepts, if you look a bit closer, you will find deeper meaning anchored in Biblical principles that come straight from the heart of our creator Himself. The deeper look at the ultimate benefits of "REST-oration" can be found in the Jewish tradition of Sabbath. For centuries, Jews and Christians have set aside a day consecrated to God for the purpose of rest and worship, bringing spiritual enrichment and perspective.

Our modern-day concept of sabbatical is drawn from the same root word as Sabbath. If you look into it a bit, you will find a tie-in with the number seven. Colleges award professors with a sabbatical every seventh year. Sabbath falls on the seventh day of the week. I (Kim) can take a hint. I was born in the seventh month—July. Right as this book goes to print,

I will turn forty-seven—and I am giving myself quite a reward. As of this year, I am officially instituting July, the seventh month, as my self-imposed sabbatical.

Okay, perhaps you think we are crazy. You don't have to take off a month or even a week, but our insights around celebration and restoration have convinced us of one thing. Regular periods of unplugged time to renew and celebrate are essential to holding onto your vision, staying fresh in your creative innovation, and ultimately connecting every accomplishment back to the most important thing—the person you are becoming, and those you are taking along on the journey.

Get out that hammock, the one that has been hanging in the garage, collecting dust, since your kids left for college. Lay back (if you are a true workaholic, we strongly suggest you do this in the middle of your work day), stare at the sky, and wait—wait for your next idea to come, your next vision flight plan to emerge, or for your weary body to fall asleep and awake RESTored and full of life.

Vision is a high-impact sport. Your life of vision will leave you bruised and battered as you press through those tension points, where others back off and settle for mediocrity.

Remember that every elite-level athlete knows when to train and when to rest for optimal performance.

When you look at the cover on this book—at the guy breaking the winning tape with his own chest—smile, and remind yourself that your time for celebration has come. Restoration will effortlessly emerge out of celebration; and out of that powerful rest will flow energy for accomplishment that perfectly matches what is required for you to cross that finish line and break the tape with your own chest ... *your moment of victory.* The place where you drop to one knee, gather your confidence and determination, and get back in the race—determined to press through any and every tension point that stands to threaten your destiny.

We trust that *The Tension Point* has more fully equipped you and inspired your race. Now get out there and *run, run, run.* It is now up to you to break through to where you want to be!

CHAPTER DISCOVERIES

- The true visionary always has multiple flight plans (visions, dreams) working simultaneously.

- One key to motivation is to keep striving to be better than you are.

- The greatest opportunity held by any visionary is the chance to lead others into a life of vision.

- Visionary Leaders are empowering, motivating people of influence who value the potential in others.

- Value and self-respect are at the heart of celebration.

- Honor who you are over what you accomplish.

- Celebrate prematurely with a "potential party" where you take time to declare and honor something you plan to achieve and your faith in yourself to see it through.

Tension Points

- Settling for life as it is

- Failing to file a new flight plan as one vision comes near completion

- Failing to see yourself as a leader

- Refusing to duplicate yourself and your efforts

- Misinterpreting status, power, and position for true leadership

- Failing to value the high-impact practice of celebrating

- Setting up the wrong rewards or refusing the rewards when they come along

- Celebrating accomplishment rather than potential … delaying the reward

- Living a life that is void of daily celebration

Activate Your Coaching Breakthrough

- Take one of your current goals and set it in the context of the big picture of vision. If your goal is to increase revenue by a certain percentage or to take more vacations, take time to assess the benefits that will come and how that single goal will allow you to reach your desired destination.

- Identify an area of life or work that feels doomed to mediocrity. For example, you feel handicapped by limited technology skills; maybe you have a relationship challenge. Write out a plan for expanding that area from good to extraordinary.

- Write out your highest vision for your life and business. Ask yourself how your life and behavior would change if that vision was fulfilled today. Now ask yourself, "How can I begin living today as if that vision is already my reality?"

- Remember, leading is impacting. Choose one person per week for the next month and invest in them in positive ways.

- What is your favorite way to celebrate? Think of something you plan to accomplish this year and throw a "potential party." Go ahead and be bold—gather a friend or two and celebrate as you declare what you will be achieving. Ask your friends to share what they hope to do as well.

- Who is someone in your life that may feel overlooked or undervalued? Find a way to celebrate them and their great potential today.

Conclusion

By Kim Fletcher

One of my best friends is Lorrie Lawrence. Lorrie is a gifted entrepreneur, speaker, trainer, leader, and minister who holds the impressive credential of former Air Traffic Controller in the Navy. As this book was coming to a close, she and I sat over coffee and discussed that role and the responsibility of guiding air traffic to safe and simultaneous landings.

As a Life Coach, Speaker, Trainer and Author, I could relate to her insights from the tower. Here are a few of the highlights from our conversation. As you take a glance, think about how these observations relate to the life of a person who longs to live out their ultimate vision(s).

As Harold's background as a pilot will invite you to see yourself "piloting" your unique life and business visions, place yourself in these lessons as the pilot, while picturing the Tower Crew as your vision keeping supports and accountability partners.

Lessons Lorrie learned from her time in the Tower

(my thoughts in italics):

• The only way the Tower crew can benefit the pilots, and keep order in the air and on the ground, is if the pilots are willing to heed their instruction. *Some of you will read this book, and a few of you will live it. The difference will be those who are "coachable."*

• Communication is the main skill for the Air Traffic Controller. They are required to learn phraseology, which allows them to communicate quickly, clearly, and effectively with each other and with the pilots. *Be careful as you choose whom you will share your ultimate visions with and be specific with your accountability team as you communicate where you are headed.*

• You must work as a team, with every member of the crew knowing and respecting the specific boundaries and responsibilities over their particular domain of air space. If one crew member crosses over into another territory, miscommunication and omissions could have devastating results. *Know your role and responsibilities as you activate your visions, and know the role of your supports.*

• Crew in the Tower must be on the same frequency with each other and with the pilots. It is important to build your support team with individuals you communicate well with. *You need to all be on the same "frequency," determined to live a life of vision in all areas.*

• There is no room for ambiguity. Each pilot must know when he or she is being addressed: "Alpha, Charlie, Delta 165." *Once you begin connecting each day to your greatest dreams, stay alert to incoming messages from your support team, your industry, your network. Staying well informed will allow you to be proactive, rather than reactionary, as you move forward.*

• The pilots in flight can hear their own specific instructions, as well as the background communication between the Tower and the other pilots. This allows each pilot access to the bigger picture, strengthening teamwork and positioning them to watch out for each other while in the air. *Your journey toward your ultimate destinations will uniquely position you to be a mentor and a support to others. Refuse to get "selfish" in this process of crafting and living out your vision. At its best, the life of vision is a life of community, connecting us to great individuals who fuel our passions and excellence.*

• While the pilot is fully responsible for his own instruments and what he does with the instruction received from the Tower, the Tower relays critical information for his safety and for the fulfillment of the flight plan. The Tower has the only view of the "invisible," as the radar gives them a bird's-eye perspective, as if they are perched high above the air activity, directing and coordinating multiple planes as they share the same air space. *Your trusted supports can see things objectively in you and your actions. Keep your heart open to receive their insights and direction. Remember: the greatest vision keeper you will ever enlist is God Himself. I truly believe that He is the author of every great vision that brings fulfillment, healing, restoration, and greater good to the world through His people. He has a perspective of your life that exceeds your own. He can see and communicate direction, wisdom, and strategic action steps that you will need for turning your greatest dreams into reality.*

As I marveled at the incredible skill and responsibility, which rests on the shoulders of the Air Traffic Controllers, Lorrie simply said, *"You don't have to be that smart, you just have to be coachable."*

Well, there it is: our ultimate *Tension Point* challenge to you, our reader. The life of vision is not reserved for the elite, intellectually superior, financially wealthy, or the powerful leaders. It is reserved for anyone with the heart to dream and the determination to be "coachable." If you have a vision, large or small, with passion driving you forward and a strong support team surrounding you, you can achieve more with your life and possess greater fulfillment than you ever dreamed possible.

Yes, there will be some invisible walls of tension to press through along the way, but the clearing, the view, the freedom, and the adventure that waits on the other side will be well worth the effort. Those who fail to press through gain regrets while those who refuse to settle for status quo attain their highest hopes, and learn how to be vision keepers for those who come along behind and beside them.

Take these lessons and suggestions here and you WILL break through to where you want to be.

ACKNOWLEDGEMENTS

by Harold Elmore

To: **Maryanna Young** and the great team at *Aloha Publishing*. All of you gave your heart and soul to produce a great book. Thank you!

My former employer, **Jerry Gibson**, for his mentoring and coaching about business and success and for believing in me.

My daughter, **Kristin Elmore Smith**, for living a life that is a great example of this book.

My very special sister, **Elaine Krieger**, for always being there for me.

Several great leaders who have helped in various ways with motivational materials, life lessons and seminars including **Zig Ziglar, Mitchell Tolle, Jim Rohn, Brian Tracy,** and **John G. Miller.**

And many friends that encouraged me along life's path including: **Jon Estes, Larry Hardin, Mike Bullington, Michael Ledford,** and **Bill Moser.**

And, most important to my wife since 1988 – **Donna** – Thanks for saying, *"Yes."* Also, many thanks for all your typing of material and helping with my schedule and for your great attitude during this process. Donna, you will always be my best friend and motorcycle riding partner.

ACKNOWLEDGEMENTS

by Kim Fletcher

Kay Fletcher, my ultra-cool Mom, for all of her practical support and powerful love during this time-consuming project.

My dear friend and owner of *Aloha Publishing*, **Maryanna Young**, for providing years of support as I have developed professionally in the areas of life coaching, speaking, and writing. Your imprint is seen in every area of my life.

My coaching clients who have given me my greatest education through the sharing of life experiences, a gift, which can never be contained or expressed by a textbook. Thank you for sharing your stories and your trust, as we have ventured together into becoming and living out all we were created to be.

My greatest inspirations in life, the individuals who are living out this concept of *"Breaking Through"* every *"Tension Point"* to attain excellence and influence: **Judy Siegle** at judysiegle.com, **Lorrie Lawrence** at transformations.com, **Anthony Majok** at southernsudanvoiceofhope.com, **Joni Eareckson Tada** at joniandfriends.org, **Mercy Hope** at FaithTalks.com, **Jan Shaffer, Liberty Barrett** at jemfriends. org, and **Stephanie Carrillo** at kimfletcherassociates.com.

To **my associate coaches and speakers** who inspire me to greatness. Meet and learn how you can partner with our extraordinary team at: kimfletcherassociates.com.

Melissa Gibson, for your friendship and artistic contribution of photography that has impacted our cover and our website.

Mercy Hope, for your friendship, practical supports during the writing of *The Tension Point,* and for your artistic contribution of our cover and interior design.

Glory Savage, my friend and webmaster for creating thetensionpoint.com and kimfletcherassociates.com. Your kindness, integrity and skill will surely make your web design business a great success!

Kelly Antonczak of *Aloha Publishing* for your friendship and hours spent refining the concepts contained in this book … and for living them out and changing the lives of those around you in the process.

Also for our editor, **Amy Bruggemann.**

To my friend and the wife of my co-author, **Donna Elmore**, for patiently supporting this process, and for the gift of your faith and friendship.

Most importantly, thank you to the **Lord Jesus** who has downloaded many concepts, principles, and gifts to my spirit. I live to make your name famous and to direct back all of the credit and honor to the One who speaks, writes, and lives through me. There is no ultimate power or lasting influence in any written word unless it is inspired by YOU!

ABOUT THE AUTHORS

HAROLD ELMORE is an award-winning entrepreneur, business trainer, and former pilot. His greatest passion is condensing his vast experience into powerful strategies and systems that will allow any individual to achieve success in business while achieving fulfillment in life. In *The Tension Point,* Harold condenses years of experience, honest struggles and vast successes into practical strategies that serve to enhance the journey of any individual who is ready to explode beyond the eight-to-five box, to achieve significance and success by their own design. He and his beautiful wife, Donna, can be seen on their bright yellow Harley Davidson on the scenic highways across the country.

KIM FLETCHER is a Master Life Coach, three-time Author, and Professional Speaker. Her extensive background as a Physical Therapist, Disability Advocate, College Instructor, and entrepreneur have equipped Kim with unprecedented skills in the areas of facilitating freedom, unleashing potential, and creating lasting change for clients globally. Individuals and groups who are compelled to personal and professional integrity and excellence refer to their partnership with Kim as a great investment. *The Tension Point* concept emerged out of a decade spent coaching clients to break through the invisible walls that separate them from their ultimate personal and professional lives. Kim works globally and relaxes at her favorite beach in Maui, Hawaii.

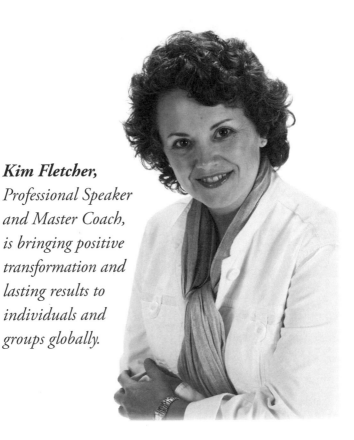

Kim Fletcher,
Professional Speaker
and Master Coach,
is bringing positive
transformation and
lasting results to
individuals and
groups globally.

CONTACT KIM DIRECTLY TO LEARN HOW A
PARTNERSHIP WITH HER AND HER ASSOCIATES
COULD IMPACT YOUR PERSONAL AND
PROFESSIONAL DEVELOPMENT.

828.327.6702
KIMFLETCHERCOACH@AOL.COM
KIMFLETCHERASSOCIATES.COM